ZECHARIAH

The Quintessence of Old Testament Prophecy

ZECHARIAH

The Quintessence of
Old Testament Prophecy

Walter C. Kaiser, Jr.

Lederer Books
An imprint of
Messianic Jewish Publishers
Clarksville, MD 21029

Cover design by Lisa Rubin,
Messianic Jewish Publishers
Graphic Design by Yvonne Vermillion,
MagicGraphix.com
Editing by George A. Koch

ISBN 978-1-7339354-9-4

Published by:
Lederer Books
An imprint of Messianic Jewish Publishers
6120 Day Long Lane
Clarksville, MD 21029

Distributed by:
Messianic Jewish Publishers & Resources
Order line: (800) 410-7367
lederer@messianicjewish.net
www.MessianicJewish.net

Table of Contents

Introduction to Zechariah

The Importance of Zechariah

Martin Luther called the Old Testament book of Zechariah *Ausbund der Propheten*, "The quintessence of Old Testament prophecy." Because this prophecy deals with both the first and second coming of Messiah, it has a privileged spot in the heart and lives of believers. George L. Robinson described the book of Zechariah as "the most Messianic, the most truly apocalyptic and eschatological of all the writings of the Old Testament."

Some of the great Messianic passages in Zechariah include: The "Branch," who is the servant (3:8); the "man," who is the "Branch"; The "King-Priest" (6:13); his triumphal entry into Jerusalem on Palm Sunday (9:9); the True Shepherd (11:4–11), the betrayal of the true Shepherd (11:12–13); the "piercing" of the Lord (12:10); and his second arrival in glory (14:4).

These prophesies and more are a particularly accurate description of the Messianic prophecies about Yeshua and his second coming. Therefore, this is one of the two main reasons why this text, which is next to the last book of the twelve Minor Prophets, should be esteemed as being especially valuable to believers. The other reason why this book should be so honored among believers is because the light it sheds on the last days of this earth's history, just before the great and terrible "Day of the LORD."

To further illustrate both contentions, note Zechariah's terse style as he describes the person and ministry of Messiah. He notes in detail the thirty pieces of silver that will be paid for our Lord's betrayal (11:13), the spear that "pierced" Yeshua's side (12:10), the "Man" on the cross who is God's equal (6:12), the day in which the Lord of Glory's "feet will stand once again on the Mount of Olives" (14:4), and the day when ADONAI "will be king over the whole earth" (14:9). Zechariah's Messianic prophecies are second only to those of the prophet Isaiah in distinctiveness and elaborate description. This is one reason some say this book is the most difficult in the Bible to interpret.

Nevertheless, Zechariah is used most extensively in the rest of the Bible. For example, one commentator noted that the passion narratives of the New Testament Gospels quoted from Zechariah 9–14 more than from any other portion of the Old Testament. Especially prominent in the message of the early Church were the texts of Zechariah 9:9–10; 11:12; 12:10 and 13:7–9.

But just as important for the believer is the light Scripture sheds on the events of the last days. Zechariah reports that a Jewish remnant will return to Israel in a condition of unbelief, just as they are doing even now. They will face a fiery furnace of suffering and tribulation as the final siege of Jerusalem takes place and they are confronted for the last time with the confederated armies of the Gentile nations. But that will also be the occasion for the victorious interruption of this new holocaust as our Lord dramatically arrives for a second time on the Mount of Olives. Then will he speak "peace" to the nations, and Israel will finally enter the long-delayed benefits of his priestly mission.

The Author of Zechariah

Zechariah means "ADONAI remembers." He is the central figure of a group of three post-exilic prophets—Haggai, Zechariah and Malachi. Zechariah's book is the longest and most frequently quoted books of the twelve Minor Prophets. In fact, there are 71 quotations or allusions to the book of Zechariah in the New Testament; one-third of these appear in the Gospels and 31 in Revelation. Amazingly, Zechariah is second only to the prophet Ezekiel in his influence on the book of Revelation.

Here are the 31 allusions in the book of Zechariah to Revelation:

The Prophet	Revelation
1:6	10:7; 11:18
1:8	6:2, 8; 19:11
2:1, 2	11:1
2:10	21:3
3:1	12:10
4:2	4:5
4:3	11:4
4:10	5:6
4:11–14	11:4
6:2	6:4, 5
6:3	6:2, 8
6:5	7:1
6:6	6:2, 5
12:3	21:25
12:10	1:7
12:11	16:16
12:12	1:7
12:14	1:7
14:7	21:25; 22:5
14:8	22:1
14:9	11:15; 19:6
14:11	19:11; 22:3

There are some 30 different individuals named Zechariah in the Old Testament, but the author of this book was "the son of Berechiah, the son of Iddo" (1:1), which meant he was from a priestly family, as were the prophets Jeremiah (1:1) and Ezekiel (1:3). Nehemiah speaks of an Iddo, who as a head of a priestly family returned from the Babylonian captivity to Judah (Neh. 12:4, 16). Assuming this is the same Iddo, Zechariah came from the priestly tribe of Levi. This would mean his father Berechiah died at an early age before he could succeed his father Iddo in the cycle of serving priests. This made it necessary for Zechariah to step up and fill the vacancy in the cycle of priests in the Temple according to the set schedule. Moreover, the text does suggest that Zechariah was a young man: Hebrew *na`ar* (2:4), "boy," "lad," "youth." The meaning of this term is given in 1 Samuel 17:33, where Saul said of David, "You are but a youth." Jeremiah had also complained that he was a mere "child" (Jer. 1:6). So Zechariah could not have been more than 30 years of age according to the *usus loquendi* ("spoken use") here.

The first eight chapters were written in Zechariah's younger years, and they date on our Julian calendars to November 520 BCE (1:1). This means that 18 years had elapsed since the year Cyrus of Persia (538) had given this Jewish remnant permission to return to Judah. The last six chapters (9–14) were most likely written in Zechariah's old age. If so, these would have been the days when the Persian Empire (today Iran) was waning, coming sometime after the death of King Darius in 485. These changes in the political circumstances of the Persian Empire and the changes in the age of the prophet may well account for the differences in style, outlook and themes in chapters of 9–14 compared to chapters 1–8.

Style and Unity of Zechariah

Like Haggai, Zechariah's book also has four main sections:

   I.   A Call for God's People to Repent – 1:1–6

   II. A Series of Eight Night Visions – 1:7–6:15

   III. A Question on Observing a Set of National Fast Days – 7:1–8:23

   IV. A Prophecy About the Future Divided into Two "Burdens" – 9:1–14:21

The eight night-visions in chapters 1–6 form a chiasm. The eight visions are organized as follows: a, b, b, c, c, b, b, a. That is, the first and eighth visions share the same concerns, while the fourth and fifth give the theological climax to all eight visions. The call to repentance in the first introductory message is likewise repeated at 7:4–14 and 8:9–17.

Add to those observations the fact that the conclusion of section two in 8:20–23, with the nations flocking to Jerusalem to be with the Lord of Hosts, is repeated at the conclusion of section 4, with the nations finally with the Lord in Jerusalem (14:16–20), and we have another inclusion, i.e., a bracketing of the sections with the end of each being indicated. But it is now time to turn to the text of Zechariah itself.

Lesson 1

A Call for God's People to Repent
Zechariah 1:1–6

We Must Repent if We Wish to Experience All of God's Blessings – 1:1–3

G. L. Robinson called 1:1–8 "one of the strongest and most intensely spiritual calls to repentance to be found in the Old Testament." It had been some 18 years since King Cyrus issued his famous decree that allowed the Jewish captives to return home to Judah. In addition, he gave them materials to rebuild the Temple of the LORD in 538 BCE Thus, in this introductory message alone, Zechariah gave four summons to repent just three months before God gave the eight night visions of what was going to happen in 1:7–6:8. This word from the Lord came in the "eighth month" (1:1; approximately our month of November), which followed a similar call "to turn back to God," a call that also came from his colleague, the prophet Haggai, which originated in the sixth month (Hag. 1:1) and in the "seventh month" (Hag. 2:1). After Zechariah preached in the eighth month, Haggai followed with two more messages in the "ninth month," both on the same day (Hag. 2:10, 20), for a total active ministry of five months.

Some 50,000 Jews had returned under the governorship of Zerubbabel and the High Priesthood of Joshua in 536. Immediately they got busy rebuilding the Temple. But discouragement settled in as the older generation, who had seen Solomon's Temple, expressed sorrow over how small this new temple was compared to the size of Solomon's. Work came to a halt until 520. God sent two prophets, Haggai and Zechariah, to rouse the people to finish building the Temple that had been abandoned for 16 long years. Thus, Zechariah's task was to convince the people to both see the work to its completion and accompany that work with a spiritual change of heart and life.

To accomplish this needed encouragement, God sent his word to Zechariah to give to the people his message in 520, during the reign of the Medo-Persian king Darius. What is significant is that the prophecies of God do not carry the dateline of one of the kings of Judah, for we now enter the times of the Gentiles. In fact, Jerusalem, Yeshua said, would be trodden under foot until the times of the Gentiles were fulfilled (Lk. 21:24).

The message to Zechariah began with an emphatic statement about God's deep anger with the ancestors of the nation of Israel (v. 2). It was high time Judah recognized the Lord "has been very angry with [their] fathers."

Such a beginning for this message arouses some modern protests and a false comparison: "The God of the New Testament is a God of love and mercy!" Why then does the Old Testament focus on divine wrath? This complaint misses the fact that both testaments affirm God's infinite holiness, which cannot tolerate sin and evil in any form. Moreover, it is a sign of a sick society when we are only willing to listen to the announcements of God's love or compassion and we get upset when the same Lord declares his wrath against sin. God is indeed "slow to anger" (Nah. 1:3), but his patience with us as persons who are the objects of his love and grace should not be read as a weakness or a hesitancy to deal with sin (2 Pet. 3:9). Both testaments affirm God's wrath as well as his love (Ex. 34:6–7; Deut. 7:7–11; John 3:16, 36).

Verse 2 gives a triple emphasis to God's anger against sin. By now it was also clear that the Lord was exceedingly displeased with Judah, for they had now remained in captivity in Babylon for some 70 years. The point of God's displeasure could hardly be lost on the hearts and minds of the captives.

The straightforward solution to the nation's current sin situation was to "return" (v 3) to the Lord. No other single word epitomized the total message of all the prophets better than "return" (Hebrew t'shuvah) to the Lord. Here was the single most important prerequisite to receiving any of God's blessings. It was a call to reverse our direction of following our own goals, aims and purposes in life. Our Lord still wants us to do a 180-degree turn and make his goals, aims and purposes part of our own lives.

I learned this lesson in another realm the hard way. In 1952, I had just finished my first year at Wheaton College, and my parents had driven out from Philadelphia to Illinois to drive me home for my summer job. This was before the interstate system had been completed. After I finished an evening concert singing with the College Chapel Choir, we headed east on Route 30, the old Lincoln Highway. Sometime past midnight, in western Ohio, I took my turn driving. I encountered a poorly marked construction detour. Early the next morning, I noticed the town of Bryan, Ohio. It seemed identical to the Bryan we had passed through overnight. Then the terrible reality set in: I'd reversed direction at the detour and gone back over the miles we already covered. So I had to turn around and cover the state of Ohio again!

That is what Zechariah was calling for. He wanted a "U-turn" theology. Thus, the earmark of all God's true messengers was this summons to reverse direction and turn back to the Lord! The concept of "turning" or "returning" is not an abstract teaching; it is very personal and real. Repentance from sin is the very prerequisite of any fellowship with God (1 John 1:9). It is so important that Zechariah refers to repentance three times (in the Hebrew text). It is just the way the prophet Isaiah (55:6–7) presented it as well:

> Seek the LORD while he may be found, call upon him while he is near. Let the wicked forsake his way, and the unrighteous man his thoughts; let him return to the LORD, and he will have mercy on him; and to our God, for he will abundantly pardon."

Joel used the same offer:

> Turn to me with all your heart … rend your heart, and not your garments; return to the LORD your God, for he is gracious and merciful, slow to anger and of great kindness." (2:12–13).

That is how Malachi also put it:

> Return to me and [or: so that] I will return to you. (3:7)

Moreover, the title "LORD of Hosts" designated our Lord as ruler over the whole universe. He was sovereign over the armies of heaven and earth alike (Judg. 5:14; 1 Sam. 17:45; 1 Kgs. 22:19; Luke 2:13; Rev. 19:14). This title for our Lord was a favorite in post-exilic times. It was used 261 times in the Old Testament from 1 Samuel on, yet it was used 91 times by Haggai, Zechariah and Malachi (14, 53, and 24 times, respectively).

We Must Be Responsive to the Lessons of History if We Do Not Wish to Be Destroyed – 1:4

Four times the "fathers" figure in the brief text of verses 1–6. The previous generations are cited for their negligence, inattentiveness, and disobedience. The "fathers" had sinned in their "evil ways" and "evil deeds." The evil ways denoted a direction and a mindset; i.e., a path or a tendency that always seemed to go off on the evil option. The evil deeds, on the other hand, signaled that Judah's actual practices and activities were in themselves also evil. Thus, some will merely lean in the direction of evil, but others will actually do the works of evil. Both sins, however, are condemned here.

The former prophets had likewise presented this same truth, for they too had urged the people of God: "Turn please." The Hebrew word for "please" is more than just a grace note added to the text. It marked the earnestness of the former prophet's appeal to them.

So, what if anything, do we learn from the history about Judah's past failures? Is history, as Henry Ford suggested, just "bunk"? But if history is real, then it sure is risky to ignore its lessons. If we would respond as God wants us to, we will not have to relearn history the hard way.

We Must Realize How Brief the Time and Opportunities Are if We Wish to Do Anything Positive for God – 1:5

To talk about the prophets and the earlier generation from a different perspective, note that the times in which both lived did not last forever; it was a brief time! One might have thought that both the prophets and even earlier generations would be around for ages, for so it appeared—especially from the perspective of the prophets' constant admonitions. But look how fleeting life turned out to be! Both the prophets and the fathers had long since passed away. So will we all, in time. Now is the time to act if we wish to please God. There is so little time, so it is critical that we quickly do something to the glory of God, for we do not know how many days we may still have to respond.

We Must Count on the Unchangeableness of Our Lord's Word if We Wish to Do Anything That Lasts – 1:6

The prophets seemed fragile and temporary in their stay on this earth, but not God's Word. The word that begins verse 6, "Nevertheless," points to the permanence, immutability and unchangeableness of the Word. God's Word and purpose will endure forever, whereas his prophets lasted only so long. We must learn to distinguish between the transience of even the best of God's servants versus the abiding veracity and eternality of the message of his prophets. Over the years we have heard of many startling revelations concerning the moral and doctrinal failures of some of the more famous televangelists and pastors of our day, but our trust must not be in these mortals; it must instead be in our Lord and his Word.

The Lord asks: "Did not my words overtake your fathers?" (v. 6c). What a graphic picture: God's words functioned like a patrol officer who spots a speeder, turns on his flashing lights and overtakes the speeding car as he pulls it to the curb. Similarly, the word of God will "curb" us and our culture as it pulls up alongside us and nails us for the infractions we have committed.

Interestingly, the word "overtake" is a direct quote from Deuteronomy 28:15,45. There God had warned that his Word would "overtake" us if we tried to run away from him, for his Word endures and is operative forever (1 Pet. 1:25). It is like a hammer that breaks the rock to pieces (Jer. 23:29). He would either do what he threatened, or what he promised.

The plan and purposes of God would be carried out both for Judah and for the nations. God would do "just as he had determined to do to us" (v. 6d). No one would be able to say, "What have you done?" (Dan. 4:35d). God would do as he pleased, and no one would be able to stop or frustrate him in his plans. His "words" and "statutes" were the summaries of his requirements that were embodied in his own covenants.

Conclusions

1. God's Word is the most sure and secure basis for all our actions and responses if we really want to live. What God has said he would do—and he has brought judgment to all—unless a generation turned back to him in repentance of their sins.

2. It is important that there exist both a personal and a national repentance if we are to enjoy the blessing of our God once again.

3. While there exists externals symbols of repentance such as the use of sackcloth (Jon. 3:6, 8; Neh. 9:1; Dan. 9:3; Joel 1:8; Isa. 58:5) and the sitting in ashes (Isa. 58:5; Dan. 9:3), it is most important that we rend our hearts, not just our garments or outward demeanor (Joel 2:13).

4. Let us confess our sins and turn 180 degrees to face the Lord who is the author and finisher of our faith.

Lesson 2

A Series of Eight Night-Visions
Zechariah 1:7–17

Three and a half months after Zechariah gave his initial message in 1:1–6, and two months after Haggai gave his final two messages (Hag. 2:10–19, 20–23), Zechariah was given eight night-visions on that same "twenty-fourth day." They make up the entire second section of this four-section prophecy from God. Five months earlier, God had stirred up the spirit of Zerubbabel the governor, the spirit of Joshua the High Priest, and the spirit of all the people, through the preaching of Haggai the prophet, so the work of rebuilding the house of God had begun immediately (Hag. 1:14, 15).

The eight visions together exhibit what is called a chiastic pattern, where the eight visions are paired off in groups of two. The first and eighth visions strongly resemble each other, while visions two and three also show a strong combination of working on the same theme, as do visions six and seven. The fourth and fifth visions form the central climax to the whole series of night revelations from God. The resulting chiastic pattern looks like this:

    a. 1:7–17 Waiting in the Calm Before the International Storm
      b. 1:18–21 Watching the Nations Punish One Another
      b. 2:1–13 Expecting the Gory of God on Earth
        c. 3:1–10 Symbolizing the Removal of Sin All in One Day
        c. 4:1–14 Receiving God's Spirit for Doing His Work
      b. 5:1–4 Purging Evil from Israel
      b. 5:5–11 Removing Wickedness from Israel
    a. 6:1–15 Executing Judgment on the Nations

In addition to the chiastic pattern, there is one other noteworthy pattern in these visions. Typically, each begins with what Zechariah "saw," followed by, "What are these for?" Or "What do these mean?" The vision concludes with an explanation: "Then the angel of the LORD answered and said…" The pattern is that the vision is seen, asked about and interpreted.

Interestingly, these visions addressed themselves more directly to the prophet's mental and spiritual sight than they impacted the hearing of his ears, even though these visions were called "the word of the Lord" (Zech. 1:7b). Nevertheless, the pictures seen in the spirit with their interpretations were called God's word, for by means of the pictures and their meanings God's will and purposes for the future were made known.

We should not be thrown off by God's use of visions to communicate his will and purposes, for Scripture often tells us that God would use "various means" (Heb. 1:1), including a "vision" or a "dream" and other means of revelation (Num. 12:6). Thus, that is what God did for Zechariah in rapid succession one night. Though each vision was complete in itself, together they formed a substantial picture of Israel's future that would close with our Lord completing his kingdom. Let's look at the first vision.

In Granting the Vision of His Plan for the Future – 1:7–8

This first vision also begins with a dateline as did 1:1, but here it was more specific by noting the very day on which the vision was given, "the twenty-fourth day." As noted earlier, this day had its own importance!

The central figure in this vision was the rider on the red horse. He was "standing among the myrtle trees in a ravine." Right behind him there were the "red, brown and white horses" (v. 8). As the text uses a Hebrew participle, it would be fair to assume the riders of these horses had been in the very act of riding at the time of the vision.

The natural first question is: Who is that "man" on the red horse? He is identified in v. 11 as none other than the *Malak ADONAI*, i.e., the "angel of the LORD," our Lord Yeshua, who here appears in the form of a "man." But some commentators are not convinced of the equation of the two names for the same person, for they argue that if the "Angel of the LORD" in v. 11 was the same as the "man" in v. 8, then the rider on the red horse would have been represented as standing opposite the other horses, and they would not have been represented as standing "behind him."

But the text does not say these other horses were "behind him" when giving their report, for they would have turned their faces toward the "man" when speaking to him. Moreover, if the "man" and the "angel of the LORD" are two different individuals, then the text would have begun with the "angel of the LORD" as the one who was mentioned first, as the other being would have been inferior to "the angel of the LORD."

As for other symbolism, most agree that the "myrtle trees" (v. 8b) are Israel. This lowly, fragrant myrtle usually grew in the shady valley, or ravines, away from the natural gaze of the world powers. It has dark-green leaves, delicate star-like flowers and edible dark berries. The myrtle, Hebrew *Hadassah*, became a favorite name for Jewish women, including Esther.

The myrtles in this vision were said to be "in a ravine" (Hebrew *bammetsullah*), as Psalms 88:6, 107:23–24 render it. Accordingly, "in the deep" could well be a figure for the waves of trouble that had overwhelmed Israel in her captivity in Babylon, or in a larger sense it could represent the abyss-like power of the Gentile nations. Israel had already been overtaken by the "times of the Gentiles" when Jerusalem would be trodden down under foot.

Another symbol in this vision concerned the horses' variegated colors, which may have indicated that the mission of God would be mixed. If that is so, then "red" would stand for God's judgment, perhaps of war; "white" would stand for mercy and peace, and "brown" ("sorrel, speckled," "dappled," "tawny" or "reddish-brown") would represent a combination of the works of God in the days to come.

All these symbols and persons were parts of God's plan, but at the time, none of his final plans for Israel or the nations had yet begun to take place!

In Granting the Interpretation of the Vision – 1:9–12

If we had been there, we would have asked the same thing the prophet did: "What are these?" (v. 9). He was told directly what the multicolored horses meant by the man standing among the myrtles: "They are the ones whom the LORD has sent throughout the earth" (v. 10b). The Lord had sent them to "patrol" (Hebrew Hithpael form of *halak*, "to go [back and forth]," "to walk about" or "walk up and down" throughout the earth). The scope of their reconnoitering was over the entire earth, not just through the Persian Empire, which existed from the Hellespont in the west to the Indus River in the east and from the Caucasus up in the north to Egypt in the south.

However, the report that all was "at rest" was a disappointing and disconcerting evaluation of the state of affairs on planet earth! These riders had found the whole world "quiet," another participle denoting that this was an ongoing situation—the world was "at peace" (v. 11). There was a respite from war; all the world was quiescent!

What was wrong with such a report, we might ask? Don't mortals wish for peace and not war? How could this have been disappointing? The answer is, there was no sign that the time for the redemption of Judah and Jerusalem had come. The prophet Haggai had concluded his ministry a short time ago with the prediction (Hag. 2:21–22) that God would "shake the heavens and the earth" and "shatter the power of foreign kingdoms." When that happened, *then* God would finally vindicate Judah by punishing the nations for their part in destroying the people of God.

This sad state of affairs led to another question: "How long will [God] withhold mercy from Jerusalem and the towns of Judah?" (v. 12). It's a fair question; the length of that time has continued to stretch from the days of the Babylonian exile, in 586 BCE, to the current moment—some two-and-a-half millennia! Despite heartening signs on the horizon, Jerusalem is still partially under the rule of a Gentile power, while perhaps as many as another seven million Jews remain scattered through the world. But the great word of encouragement in this text is the fact that the pre-incarnate Messiah, the man on the red horse, still identifies with his people and is still standing in the glen among the myrtle trees, which represent the nation of Israel. He is still interceding for them as the Angel of his Presence. He, their great High Priest, still carries the names of all Israel on his heart, just as the human High Priest carried the names of the twelve tribes on his breastplate (Exod. 28:29).

Granting Three Declarations and Giving Four Comforting Words About the Future – 1:13–17

Despite the unsettling news, v. 13 says the Lord still "spoke kind and comforting words" to them. The first of the three declarations was: "[God is] very jealous for Jerusalem and Zion" (v. 14d). His great love for Israel will never end. Seven features of the Hebrew text make it very clear that God's covenantal love for his people has not lessened, nor will it leave them in the future. These items are: (1) This message of God's abiding love and grace was to be "cried out" with full energy and certitude; "proclaim" or "herald" it to all. (2) This word came from the "Lord Almighty" himself—the "LORD of Hosts" (v. 14c). The armies from the angelic realm and those armies from earth were those who would back up this saying, for the Lord was the "LORD of Hosts/Armies." (3) "Jealous" appears, (4) in the advanced position, for that is what is to be emphasized here. The word "jealous" is from the Hebrew *qana*, a "burning passion." (5) In the Hebrew, "Jerusalem and Zion" appear as the objects of God's love, but they are once again put in the advanced position just before the adverbial idea—(6) which likewise is put in the emphatic position: "I am very jealous: (v. 14d). (7) Finally, God adds a qualifying adjective to modify the accusative: "I am *exceedingly* jealous."

Accordingly, the High and Holy God makes clear that the people of Israel are very near and dear to him. His emotions do burn with a fiery passion to even think of the possibility that his people might be in danger of being taken away from him. Yes, the Gentiles have taken Israel and dispersed them throughout the globe from time to time, but God has been aware of their mistreatment of Israel. He will one day, very soon, rise to take vengeance on Israel's foes (Ps. 132:13–14, 17–18).

14

The second declaration was this: "I am very angry with the nations that feel secure" (v. 15). As with the first declaration, so this second one used grammatical and syntactical items to emphasize God's continuous anger with the nations. His *ongoing* anger was also signaled by his use of the participle. True, God himself was "only a little angry," "but [the nations] went too far with [their] punishment" (v. 15b–c). Yes, God handed out the punishment, but the Gentile nations greatly escalated the disasters that came on Judah and Jerusalem, arousing God's anger. Assyria, Babylonia, Persia and eventually Rome used these occasions to try to destroy—because they not only hate Israel, they hate God even more! The increasingly severe pogroms and massive annihilations of Israel have grown more grotesque since the days of Antiochus Epiphanes, Hitler, Mussolini, Putin, etc. These guilty nations may seem carefree and at rest now, but divine anger will one day break out against them and culminate in the judgment for all they have done (Zech. 6:1–8).

The third declaration is more implicit, was anticipated as we concluded the second declaration: God will judge the nations that were hostile to Israel. He will judge them in righteousness before his kingdom comes to earth (Joel 3:1–4).

These three declarations are now followed by four "kind and comforting words" (v. 13). They begin in verse 16 with "therefore," a causal adverb that sums up the reasons for the announced "kind and comforting words." These words also emphatically have the "LORD of Hosts" as their direct source (v. 16a). Thus, the first word of comfort is that Messiah will personally return. This truth is put in the past or completed tense of the Hebrew verb ("I have returned"); this is a "prophetic perfect" form of the Hebrew verb, correctly rendered in English as "I will return." The Shekinah glory, the very presence of God, did historically and literally depart from the Temple of God (Ezek. 10:18–19, 23) and left Jerusalem. God went away and returned to his place (Hos. 5:15). Later, the disciples of Yeshua no longer saw him on earth (Mt. 23:38–39) and will not until his Second Coming.

The second comforting word is that God's house will be rebuilt (v. 16c). Indeed, during Haggai and Zechariah's days the Second Temple was rebuilt, but God promises a new later millennial Temple, also known as the Third Temple. Thus, the building of the Second Temple in 520 BCE was only a partial fulfillment of the "now" aspect of this prophecy, but the "not yet" part awaits the construction of the Temple that Ezekiel saw (chapters 40–42), the same building in the beautiful prophecy of Isaiah 2:2–3c...

> In the last days,
> the mountain of the LORD's Temple
> will be established as the highest of the mountains;
>> it will be exalted above the hills,
> and all nations will come and say,
>> "Come, let us go up to the mountain of the LORD.
>> to the Temple of the God of Jacob.
>> He will teach us his ways,
>> so that we may walk in his paths."

To ensure this prophecy (which is often doubted, even by believing scholars) is certain, God adds his name to this affirmation: "This is what the LORD says" (v. 16a).

The third comforting word was that Jerusalem would experience enormous growth and expansion (v. 16d). Though the city was ravaged in 586 BCE by the Babylonians, and in 70 and 132–135 CE by the Romans, this city would experience unusual urban renewal and expansion. It would be time to take a tape-measure and to stretch it out over the city, for the "stretching out" of the surveyor's measuring-line was God's symbol for the future prosperity and extension of the city.

The fourth kind and comforting word was the best of all. Despite all the historical appearances to the contrary, God would once again "comfort Zion and choose Jerusalem" (v. 17c). He would not forget his promises made long ago to his people (Ex. 33:19; Deut. 13:17[18]; Isa. 49:15). He would conclude history just as he had said he would in the beginning.

Conclusions

1. It may have seemed discouraging to hear the report that the world was at rest and carefree with no sign of the coming judgment of God for the nations' hostility to God and Israel and the conclusion to his long-promised covenant, but God's case would not rest there in Zechariah's time—God was not yet finished with his plan for history.

2. At the designated time in the plan of God, that judgment would come to the Gentile nations and deliverance would come to Israel.

3. God's love and promised choosing of Israel could be summed up in three declarations and in four kind and comforting words.

Lesson 3

Watching the Nations
Punish Each Other as Israel Expects
the Glory of God on Earth
Zechariah 1:18–2:13

In the Hebrew text, the English verses of Zechariah 1:18–21 are numbered 2:1–4, and the English verses of 2:1–13, in the Hebrew version, are numbered 2:5–17. But this slight difference is not enough to delay us.

In the first vision, we learned that the Lord was extremely angry with the nations because of their treatment of Israel. Therefore, there was a strong hint of the coming threat of judgment (1:15). In addition to this threat, there was more than just a shadow of hope for Israel's eventual reclamation of their land. But all of this brought up the question: Just how was God going to deal with Israel's enemies?

From the datelines of the prophecies in these eight night visions, it is clear that Israel had already entered "the times of the Gentiles" (Lk. 21:24). If that was so, then what chance would Israel have for any kind of rescue or deliverance, given their smallness, weakness, and sinfulness? That was precisely the question that the vision of the four horns and four smiths set out to answer in this second vision. This vision was given on the same night as the seven other visions.

Even more amazing would be the third vision, which pairs with the second, where the Lord predicts the restoration of Jerusalem. There, the Lord would describe how the city of Jerusalem would be enlarged and become the capital for the whole millennial earth. It would increase the city of Jerusalem not only in size and population, but it would also expand it in wealth, spirituality, and security. Let us consider these two visions.

We Can Expect Those Who Scattered Israel to Be Punished – 1:18–19

The message begun in the first vision continues its message of encouragement. The successive empires of the Gentile nations had raised the ire and wrath of the Lord by the way they had acted in scattering Judah, Israel, and Jerusalem (1:19). Each nation would be broken and dissipated, usually by the nation that followed it to the seat of world power.

"Horns," the pride and symbol of strength of the animals that sport them, are used figuratively here to represent the nations that bullied Israel, scattering the small nation all over the known world that day and up to the present era. The "horn" of the animals, of course, denoted the rack of bone that protruded from the head of a ram, goat, or ox. This was no doubt a borrowed figure of speech from the observed strength or destructive power seen in bulls, wild oxen, or other parts of the wild kingdom.

Examples of such usage can be seen in Jeremiah 48:25, where the "horn" of Moab was cut off, or in Psalm 75:10, where all the "horns" of the wicked will be cut off in that future day. Even David calls the Lord "the Horn of my deliverance" (Ps. 18:2). In fact, in Daniel's vision (7:24), the "ten horns" of the Gentile kingdom are "ten kings." The same identification is made in Revelation 17:12. Even the ram, which had two horns in Daniel 8:3, represented the kings of Media and Persia. Alexander the Great was described as being the conspicuous "horn" (Dan. 8:6) that grew up between the eyes of the animal symbolizing him. Thus we can conclude that the four "horns" represent four kingdoms led by their rulers.

The prophet Zechariah wanted to know who these four "horns" were. The angel, who had been "talking" to him, quickly answered: "These are the horns that scattered Judah, Israel, and Jerusalem" (1:19). Thus, the horns signified the ruling powers, or the kingdoms who had acted through their kings (Dan. 8; Rev. 17:3–12).

Their crime was that these "horns" had "scattered," "dispersed" or "winnowed" Israel, as they had routed Israel repeatedly. This extraordinarily strong verb speaks to the unmerciful sifting these nations had exercised against the people of God in their unchecked rage. However, this "sifting" did not only include the history of the pagan nations' hostile record against Israel: All eight of these night-visions belong together and were, in fact, preparatory for the work of God in setting up his kingdom in that final day that is to come! So, these four horns cover "the times of the Gentiles." Said "times" began with the destruction of Jerusalem in 586 BCE and will continue until the all the Gentiles are gathered into the Savior (Rom. 9:25).

It seems that the identity of these four great empires is best seen as the same as the four nations revealed in Daniel 2:37–45 and 7:2–8, 17–28—Babylon, Medo-Persia, Greco-Macedonian, and, though unidentified, the fourth is usually believed to be a Roman or Western power. Rabbi Kimchi named these four monarchies, as did the Targum of Jonathan. Some refrain from naming the fourth "horn," as it had not yet showed up in its full form. If it is to be equated with a Roman or Western power, note that

Rome was divided in the fifth century CE into Eastern and Western Empires as the Church split into east and west. Since we have not yet seen the ten-king confederation represented by the toes and feet of the colossus (Dan. 2:42–44; 7:7, 8, 20; Rev. 13:1), this should caution us against making firm judgments on the identity of this fourth empire/kingdom.

We Can Expect That God Will Use Each Nation to Punish Its Predecessor – 1:20–21

Next, the Lord showed Zechariah "four craftsmen" (Hebrew *harash*), who could be labeled and translated as "workmen," "carpenters," "smiths." These were skilled workers who could work in wood, stone, or metal. Accordingly, as the prophet must have seen these workers coming on the scene with the tools of their trade, ready for work, he asked the angel, "What are these coming to do?" (v. 21), rather than asking for their identity.

The Lord's answer, through the angel, was this: "These are the horns that have scattered Israel, so that no one could raise their head" (21b). The first part of the answer repeated the statement of the preceding verse. But the words he added were meant to emphasize the intensity of Israel's sorrow and suffering in the period of their trials. So severe was the punishment of these horns that it was almost impossible to lift one's head or to hold it high! That is how heavy the imposed affliction was on Israel!

Well, then, who were these "craftsmen?" The prophet did not ask about their identity either. Instead, he inquired about their function. To generally answer that question, it is possible to say that they were, at the very least, a symbol of God's judgment. They were symbols of God's use of historical imperial powers to enact his judgment on those hostile to Israel. Thus, the number "four" stands over against the four horns. The craftsmen were clearly intended to terrify the horns.

If we try to identify each craftsman, the answer is probably thus: The first is Medo-Persia, who by King Cyrus destroyed the power of Babylon; the second is a Grecian power, who under the swift attacks by Alexander the Great reduced Persia to shambles; the third is historic Rome, which in turn reduced what was left of the power of the Greco-Macedonian empire to a shadow of its former glory.

However, the fourth craftsman was the most terrible of all. This seems to be the one that Daniel described more extensively in his seventh chapter as "dreadful, terrible, and exceedingly strong with iron teeth that devoured and broke to pieces and stamped under foot, all that confronted him" (Dan. 7:24). This man was the same figure that embodied the "ten kings" or "kingdoms."

Not only were these craftsmen to terrify the horns, but they were to throw down the nation that had preceded it, as represented by the Gentile horn that had the power up to that date, for these were the nations that "had lifted up their horns against the land of Judah to scatter its people" (v. 21d). The verb "lifted up" is an active participle, indicating their persecution of the Jews had been continuous, rather than sporadic or just occasional.

It is at the point where the Gentile march of the world powers comes to its climax in strength and pride, for with amazing cruelty, the final power of the Gentile nations is finally and forever broken and cast out. Nowhere is that climax demonstrated more graphically than in Daniel 2:44–45 (and 7:13–14). To do this, someone like the Son of Man comes with the clouds of heaven to the Ancient of Days and sets up a kingdom that will never be destroyed.

This second night-vision given to Zechariah makes two important points: (1) God will not forget his covenant with Israel, and (2) they and we must not be anxious to vindicate ourselves, for even as the apostle Paul taught, "Vengeance is Mine; I will repay says the Lord" (Rom. 12:19).

We Can Expect That Our Lord's Return Will Be Glorious – 2:1–9

In this third vision, Zechariah sees a man measuring Jerusalem, a scene that evokes the reference in the first vision where "a measuring line will be stretched out over Jerusalem" (1:16; 2:1). Thus, the purpose of this third night-vision was to prophetically announce the restoration of Jerusalem in Zechariah's time and to describe a fuller fulfillment of such a restoration in the day when the city will become the capital of the whole millennial earth.

The unity of these visions is seen not only in the content and subject matter of the eight visions, but also in the fact that they were each connected with the Hebrew conjunction *waw* consecutive, which both unites them and tells a connecting story about Israel. Thus, the first night-vision announced hope for a defeated Israel, while the second vision pointed to the vindication of her foes by each new empire. The kind and comforting words of 1:13 showed God's love for the holy city (1:14) and his anger with her attackers (1:15). The second vision asserted his anger with Zion's enemies (1:15). All of this prepared the way for a description in the third vision of the way God would extend Jerusalem and prosper her.

Nothing is more prominent in this section than the thought found in verse 5: "I myself will be wall around [Jerusalem] … and I will be its glory within." The "I" is emphatic and contrary to normal Hebrew practice, the verb "to be" is this time expressed and is put in the Hebrew incomplete form, i.e., a future action of the verb. The text adds, "declares the LORD"—acting like a signature of God attached to the declaration to reinforce its authority.

The "wall of fire" reminds us of the "cloud and pillar of fire" that accompanied Israel during the days of wandering the wilderness. Moreover, it was that same cloud and pillar of fire that separated the Israelites, temporarily halted at the Red Sea, from the pursuing Egyptian army (Ex. 14:19–24).

Likewise, God's promise to be the "glory within" (Zech. 2:5b) in that future day must have brought back to Judean memories the sequential departure of the glory of God as he abandoned his people in Ezekiel's day (Ezek. 9:3; 10:19; 11:23). His glory would not be seen on earth again until our Lord returns (Ezek. 43:1–7). But what was the glory of God? It pointed to the fact and reality of God's presence, the sheer weight and gravity of the fact that he was the Lord who would be there. Only secondarily did it involve the luminous effect that his presence subsequently produced.

But this vision featured a "man with a measuring line in his hand" (2:1). This man cannot be the interpreting angel, so it must be the one already identified as "the angel of the LORD" (1:12). He is also to be equated with no one else than our Lord Yeshua, the rider on the red horse (1:18). If some object to our Lord being called a "man," Zechariah 6:12 makes it clear there is no problem, for it teaches: "Here is the man whose name is the Branch," the Messiah.

When this man was asked what he was doing, he responded that he was measuring Jerusalem. The big news was this: There would be a huge increase in the size of this city without walls (2:4). In fact, the Hebrew word used for "city" here in v. 4 is literally "plains." The identical term was used by Ezekiel (38:11) to describe people who would dwell in peace and in a place without walls, bolts or gates. Isaiah added (49:19–20): "This place is too small for us; give us more space to live in." What then shall we say in our day to the enormous number of Jewish immigrants that have flooded into Israel—some seven million Jews! What about the possible addition of the land owned previously by Lebanon, Jordan and the Gaza Strip?

Zechariah writes the rest of chapter 2 in poetry, with verses 6–13 divided into two equal stanzas, 6–9 and 10–13. Each stanza begins with the exhortation followed by the word "for." Beginning in verse 6, Zechariah addresses the exiles in Babylon, and then the people of Zion, whose return to the land of Israel acts as a symbol of the work God will do in the final day. Each of these two stanzas begins with a command and then is followed by a reason that begins, as we have said, with "for."

Verse 6 startles us with words that literally cry out, "Ho, ho!" or "Hey there, listen up!" "Flee from the land of the north!" (2:6). The prophet sounded the alarm again in v. 7: "Come, Zion! Escape you who live in the daughter of Babylon!" This echoes the same command the prophet Jeremiah gave in 51:6: "Flee from Babylon! Run for your lives! Do not be destroyed because of her sins." Jeremiah had issued the same outcry in 50:8, "Flee out of Babylon; leave the land of the Babylonians." Now, this could hardly have meant that the residents of the Babylonian exile were to flee before Babylon fell in 539 BCE, for if that were true, then why did Daniel remain in Babylon the very night the empire fell? Daniel knew the prophecies of Jeremiah, for he refers to these 70 prophesied years of Jeremiah twice in his book (Dan. 9:2; Jer. 25:12; 29:10). One would have thought that had Daniel had understood Jeremiah's prophecies to be warnings for his own day, especially after he interpreted the handwriting on the wall in Daniel 5, he would have made a beeline out of town. Thus, we do well to take these commands to refer to an eschatological event that occur in connection with the events surrounding the coming of our Lord.

Even though Babylon resided in a south-easterly direction from Judah, she (and other conquerors from that part of the world) is described repeatedly as coming from the "north" of Israel, since invading directly east, across the desert, while providing food and water for an army or a group of refugees, would be impossible. The elliptical shape of the Near East sweeping over the northern lands is how the area received the name of the "fertile crescent."

Accordingly, verses 6 and 7 are dependent of Isaiah 13–14 and Jeremiah 50–51, both of which depict the final judgment God will place on the Babylon of the future, whoever occupies that land and position at the time. Just as Israel is being re-gathered and restored to her land from all over the world, the cup of iniquity with the wine from Babylon, which would be drunk by the nations of the world, would drive them all mad (Jer. 51:6–7), and Babylon (or any place in the north, such as Russia) would not be a good place to be living at that time. That is why Zechariah urged the Jews to leave quickly. Babylon is depicted as the gold cup in the Lord's hand. By that cup the Lord made the earth drunk as they imbibed the wine Babylon had sponsored. Thus, Babylon and the nations would fall suddenly and be broken. Meanwhile, Jerusalem would be a city protected by God and the place where his glory would be displayed (2:7b).

The adverbial expression in v. 8 is most difficult to translate and interpret. Literally, it is rendered: "after glory he sent me." It seems best rendered as a description of Messiah's ministry, in which he both demonstrates and vindicates the glory of God. Add to this that Messiah was "sent" by the Father. While Messiah the Son and God the Father are One God, in the mystery of the Trinity, Messiah was "sent" (cf. Jh. 10:38, Isa. 66:1–2).

24

To further emphasize the point, the prophet warns: "Whoever touches you [Israel] touches the apple of his eye" (2:8b). Literally, the expression is "the pupil of his eye," which is one of the tenderest and most sensitive spots on the optic nerve. Zechariah here repeats what had been said in Deuteronomy 32:10, "He shielded [Israel] and cared for him; he guarded him as the apple of his eye." Here the word rendered "apple" is the "little man"—the daughter of his eye.

To back up the truth that Israel was special, the "apple of his eyes," verse 9, threatens all who would attempt any harm against Israel. God would "raise his hand" to punish all who would oppress his people. Zechariah here repeats what the former prophets had said (e.g., Isa. 10:15). That is how the nations who had plundered Israel and Judah would themselves be plundered. That is how the nations will recognize that the Lord God had indeed sent Messiah.

We Can Expect Our Lord's Future Blessings to Be Glorious – 2:10–13

Four beautiful promises are built on the vision in verses 1–6 of this chapter two. Each describes what our Lord will do when he returns to earth to rule and reign in the millennium.

The first promise was this: "Behold, I am coming, and I will live among you" (v. 10). The second arrival of our Lord is the climax to all that has preceded it in history. God has promised that he will return in like manner as the men of Galilee saw him depart in the clouds of heaven—really, visibly, and actually! He would also take up his residence in the midst of us. That was how the tripartite formula of the promise-plan of God ended: "I will be your God; you shall be my people; and I will dwell in the midst of you."

The second promise followed in v. 11: "Many nations will be joined with the LORD in that day and will become my people." Usually "my people" was reserved for the nation Israel, but in this context it refers to Gentiles, who had joined by faith a trust in the Lord to form the one people of God. The prophet Isaiah had spoken in the same manner of those Egyptians converted in the final day (Isa. 19:25). Yes, there would only be one people of God by faith, even though they all would be grafted into the one olive tree, whose roots were in the patriarchal promises and whose trunk was the nation of Israel. Verse 11 of chapter two concludes with this special work of God being the proof that the Lord God had sent his son, the Messiah. He would be vindicated to be who he had said he was!

The third promise came in verse 12, where "The LORD will inherit Judah as his possession in the holy land and will again choose Jerusalem."

This is the only time in the Bible where the promised land is called the "holy land," however it will be found under that label in the apocryphal books of Wisdom 12:3; 2 Maccabees 1:7–11. God is certainly not finished with Jerusalem yet, even though he chose it as the place for the throne of David. But this city will serve as the place for the worship of the Living God and the place from which he will teach his law in his millennial reign.

The final and fourth promise, found in verse 13, is that there will be a worldwide judgment by Messiah when he returns the second time. At that time, the Lord will "arouse himself" "from his holy dwelling" as "all mankind" are silenced by his awesome presence. Therefore, the earth is instructed to "Be still" or "be silent," for his work will be awesome and fearsome, to say the least.

Conclusions

1. God will physically return to this earth as he told the men of Galilee.

2. The hope offered to Israel and Judah is the same hope which the Church believes in. Together, Jew and Gentile will be joined together to form the one people of God by faith.

3. Jerusalem will be rebuilt and become the new world center for worship and teaching from the Lord of glory.

4. A final world judgment will come on all nations on earth as right will finally show itself, where wrong had previously often thought it was free to express itself.

5. Babylon will be judged while Israel will be delivered.

Lesson 4

Receiving God's Spirit for Doing God's Work

Zechariah 3:1–10

The third (found in 3:1–10) and fourth (found in 4:1–14) visions God gave to Zechariah form the central and a climactic point in these eight divine night revelations. Both visions deal with the problem of sin. In the third vision, however, the filth and guilt of the sin of Joshua the High Priest, representing both his own sin and the sin of the people Israel, was so foul that their sin was depicted as excrement or filthy dung splattered all over the High Priestly garments of Joshua. This immediately raised an acute problem: How can an infinitely holy God bless a people in such a reprehensible, stinky, and foul situation?

The focal point of the third vision comes in verses 8–9: "Listen, High Priest Joshua, you and your associates seated before you … are men symbolic of things to come. … I will remove the sin of this land in a single day." What a promise for those who have just been described as being so loathsome and abhorrent!

So how can a morally deficient and sinful people be made ready to appear in the presence of God, much less be said to be priests and ministers for the Holy One, who himself is without spot or any defect?

In this fourth vision, the High Priest Joshua, who had returned from the Babylonian exile with the governor Zerubbabel, stands before the "Angel of the LORD" (3:1), who was no one less that the second person of the Trinity. Unfortunately, Satan stands there as well, for he came "to accuse [Joshua]" (3:1d), a role typical of the Evil One!

The fifth vision (4:1–14) likewise deals with the sin problem as well, which, along with the fourth vision, forms the apex of this chiastic arrangement of the eight night-visions. Each will be looked at individually.

Messiah Will Intervene for Us as Our High Priest – 3:1–2

Backsliding Israel is promised restoration back to the favor of God, not because she deserved it in any sense, but because God was gracious and so forgiving of their sin. The High Priest of the people, who had returned from

Babylon sixteen years ago, was named Joshua. He, along with the small remnant of exiles, some 49,697, had come back to their homeland in Judah.

In this vision, however, Joshua was seen standing before the Angel of the Lord with Satan standing on his right side to accuse him (3:1). This angel of the Lord is the same one that Exodus 23:20–21 declared that God's name was in him. Therefore, this angel was also called the "Angel of his Face," the One the Father had sent from himself, our Lord Yeshua.

As mediator for the people, Joshua as High Priest was there to minister, for that was his task as a part of the tribe that had been separated from the people. However, Satan interrupted his work by making accusations and attempting thereby to interrupt what God was mercifully doing for the nation in forgiving them. Satan here acts in character as the sworn enemy of both God and Israel as well as of all believers—he is known as "the accuser of the brethren" (Rev. 12:10).

ADONAI, however, pleads for Israel and all who belong to him. Isaiah 50:8–9 declared:

> He who vindicates me is near. Who then will bring any charges against me? Let us face each other! Who is my accuser? Let him confront me! It is the Sovereign LORD who helps me. Who [then] will condemn me?

Again, the same teaching is in Romans 8:33–34:

> Who will bring any charge against those whom God has chosen? It is God who justifies. Who then is the one who condemns? No one. Messiah Yeshua who died ... is at the right hand of God and is also interceding for us.

It is the Lord Yeshua himself who will rebuke Satan, just as he did in Jude 9. In fact, in Jude 23, there are two more phrases that echo Zechariah 3:2 ("snatching them from the fire," Jude 23a) and Zechariah 3:4 ("clothing stained by corrupted flesh," Jude 23c). So, the source of Jude's phrases is easy to detect – they come from the Old Testament.

Our Lord does not cast off his people or forget about them just because they have stinky garments splattered with sin. It was as if they were besmirched with dung instead of sin. The question Paul asked in Romans 11:1, with its response, is just as fitting here: "Did God reject his people? By no means!" Moreover, as Amos 4:11 taught, Israel was "like a burning stick snatched from the fire" even though, at that point, they still had not returned to the Lord! It is no wonder, then, that Israel had not otherwise been destroyed by the hand of God; it was all due to his mercy.

Thus, Joshua represented the people of Israel. The nation continued to sin and deserved the judgment of God, but our Lord would not go back on his promise. He would in the end fulfill what he had promised to Abraham, Isaac, and Jacob—he could not lie or deny himself; what he had promised would come to pass!

Messiah Will Cleanse Us as Our High Priest – 3:3–4

The prophet Isaiah had taught that "All of us have become like one who is unclean, and all our righteous acts are like filthy rags" (Isa. 64:6). It is no wonder then that the angel said to those who were standing there (Zech. 3:4), "Take off his filthy clothes." This is God's answer to Satan's accusations against Israel and for all who belong to him. Our Lord longs for the removal of all the filth that sin has introduced into our lives. His grace exceeds all our sin and guilt, for he has chosen Zion as the place he loves, and he will not recant or back down on his promise to Abraham.

Instead, God will clothe Joshua with "fine/rich garments" (v. 4d). These new clothes can be nothing less than the garments of salvation and righteousness. Only then will Israel and all who believe in the Savior be attired with perfect righteousness. Joshua himself, since he was a "sign" will be re-consecrated and reinstated because of this action. No wonder the text says that the sin of that land of Israel will be "removed in one day" (v. 9d).

Messiah Challenges Us as Our High Priest – 3:5–7

The gracious work of our Lord did not stop with his act of clothing Joshua with rich garments. He also added: "put a clean turban on his head" (v. 5). Attached to it was a plate of pure gold with the engraving written on it: "Holiness/holy to the Lord" (Hebrew *qodesh l'YHWH*). That is exactly what Exodus 28:36–38 had prescribed that Aaron the High Priest was to wear:

> Make a plate of pure gold and engrave on it as on a seal: Holy to the LORD... It will be on Aaron's forehead continually so that they [believers in Israel] will be acceptable to the LORD.... that he will bear the guilt involved in the sacred gifts the Israelites consecrate.

In God's original plan, all the people who believed were to be to him a kingdom of priests (Ex. 19:6). But even though Israel declined this offer since it was too awesome to hear the voice of God directly, there was nevertheless a day when the whole nation would be called once again to be just that—a kingdom of priests to the Lord (Isa. 61:6). In fact, that day has come already in New Testament times, when the doctrine of the priesthood of believers was announced in 1 Peter 2:5 and Revelation 1:6.

At the Wedding Feast of the Lamb, the great supper of God, all believers, like Joshua the High Priest, will be arrayed in fine linen, bright and pure as our robe of righteousness (Rev. 19:6–18; Mt. 22:1–14). What a wonderful change!

At this point the Angel of the LORD, solemnly admonished Joshua with the words that came from Deuteronomy, the words given to Joshua in the conquest, and the words dying David gave to his son Solomon:

> If you will walk in obedience to me, and keep my requirements, then you will govern my house and have charge in my courts, and I will give you a place among those standing here.

The reference to God's "house" in this context meant the "people of God." Likewise, Moses was faithful in all "God's house": (Num 12:7) and that same word "house" is used again in Hebrews 3:6 —"Messiah is faithful as a Son over God's house. And we are his house."

Thus we already have the first of three rewards promised to Joshua for his obedience: he would be judge over the "house" or the "people of God" (v. 7c). The second reward to the High Priest was he would have "charge of [God's] courts" (v. 7d). He would exercise authority over the Temple and its courts. The third reward was that God would "give [him] a place among those standing there" (v. 7e). Apparently, this was the promise that in the resurrection, Joshua would have the honor of walking among the seraphim. This phrase is harder to interpret, however.

Messiah Will Deliver Us as Our High Priest – 3:8–10

Joshua and his associates are hereby declared by God to be "men symbolic of things to come" (v. 8). So the focus was not really on Joshua or those around him; no, it was to be on Messiah who would come.

Two marvelous titles of our Lord appear in verse 8: "My Servant" and "the Branch." "My Servant" is the most frequent title used for Yeshua even though we use the title "Messiah" more frequently. For example, if judged solely on the bases of the number of usages in the Bible, "Messiah," representing Yeshua, occurs only nine times out of the 39 usages of that word in the Old Testament, while "Servant" refers to Messiah some 20 times in Isaiah 41–53 alone.

The name "Branch" appears in four wonderful promises about the coming of Messiah and they give four distinct presentations of Messiah in the prophecies of Isaiah, Jeremiah, and Zechariah. The early Church Fathers loved to preach on these four presentations of Messiah as the "Branch." First of all, there was the presentation of "the Branch of David," found in Jeremiah 23:5–6, which corresponded to the gospel of Matthew's presentation of Messiah as the coming royal king (Mt. 1) from David's line. Likewise, the presentation of Messiah in Zechariah 3:8 as the "Servant," who is the "Branch," is picked up in Mark's gospel as the way to present our Lord—as one who came to serve and give his life as a ransom from many (Mk. 10:45). Zechariah 6:12 presented our Lord as the "Branch, a man," which anticipated Luke's presentation of our Lord Yeshua as the Man *par excellence*. Finally, Isaiah 4:2 talked about the "Branch of the Lord," which is the gospel-writer John's way of saying (20:31) that all the miracles he listed were to show that Yeshua is the Son of God.

In verse 9, Joshua the High Priest was told that God had set a "Stone" in front of him with seven eyes on it. These eyes spoke of God's manifold omniscience and intelligence, similar to Isaiah 11:2, where Immanuel was given the spirit of wisdom, understanding, counsel, might, knowledge, and the fear of God. In the Jewish Talmud, this stone is the "Foundation Stone," which had this engraving on it (see also Rev. 5:6).

The prophet Isaiah taught in Isaiah 28:6 that God would lay in Zion a foundation stone that was a precious cornerstone. All those who would believe in this stone would not be ashamed or in haste. Likewise, in Psalm 118:22, was it not the very stone the builders had rejected that indeed became the headstone of the corner?

But even more importantly, the key to this whole vision was that God would remove the iniquity of the whole land of Israel in "one day!" This would come as Israel repented of her sin and "all Israel" would be saved. This then leads, as one would expect, to a picture of tranquility and gladness of heart in verse 10. Now that Israel's sin has been forgiven and removed, she is fully pardoned and she rests secure with her neighbors as the days of peace return to that land.

Conclusions

1. Our God has intervened on behalf of Israel and all who have believed as his blood cleanses us from all our sin.

2. Our sins are completely removed and forgotten by a gracious and loving God.

3. In Israel's case, however, this massive event of forgiveness will come one day in the future as God climaxes history.

4. Israel and the Church must be distinguished, therefore, even if they must not be separated if they believe in Messiah.

Lesson 5

Not by Might, but by God's Spirit
Zechariah 4:1–14

This fifth vision, along with the fourth vision, stands in closest relationship to each other the central messages of the eight night-visions. In the first three, God wanted to show that he had not forsaken his people or cast them off: His "kind and comforting words" (1:13) proved the very opposite. Even though Judah was under an oppressive yoke of a series of Gentile powers, and many were still in the land of captivity, the Angel of the Covenant, the Lord himself, was in their midst pleading their cause (1:8–12). Anyone who touched Israel, "touched the apple of his eye" (2:8).

But how could a holy God do such marvelous things to such a rebellious and persistently sinning people? The third vision answered that question by arguing that such kindness would not rest on Israel's worthiness or merits, but solely on the grace of God.

Just as the fourth vision focused on Joshua the High Priest, who as representative of the people needed to be cleansed, so the fifth vision focuses on Zerubbabel who will need to complete the Temple, but not depend on his human ingenuity alone, but on the Spirit of God.

A slight pause has intervened in this series of night visions. But then in 4:1 the prophet is brought back into a spiritually wakeful state as the angel woke him up again and asked him, "What do you see?" (4:2). We are now ready for the fifth vision.

God's Work Will Be Accomplished by God's Spirit – 4:1–6

After the angel had aroused Zechariah, he inquired about what he was seeing (4:2). He answers: "I see a solid gold lamp stand with a bowl at the top and seven lamps on it with seven channels to the lamps" (v. 2b). Now this lamp stand was different from the seven-branched menorah found in later Jewish art and illustrated in Titus' memorial arch in Rome. Instead, it was composed on solid gold and no doubt formed a pedestal that had a bowl on top of this column, in which there perhaps was a flared feature that formed seven lamps, each with a pinched spout to hold seven wicks. It is not unheard-of to find lamps with seven pinches around the lips.

In addition to this seven-fluted lamp stand, Zechariah was shown "two olive trees by it, one on the right of the bowl and the other on its left" (v. 3). The meaning of these two olive trees will be clearly identified in verses 12–14, where they are equated with "the two who are anointed to serve the Lord of all the earth," i.e., Zerubbabel and Joshua.

But interestingly enough, Zechariah inquires in verses 4, 11 and 12, "What are these [trees]?" The angel is surprised that he does not know what these two olive trees (later called "olive branches" in v. 12) are. The word rendered "branches" may be translated as "clusters" of fruit as well. The angel responds, "Do you not know what these are?" (v. 5). "No," answers the prophet. He clearly knew what he knew and what he did not! In this case, he must be told if he was to interpret this vision.

But again, we are surprised that the angel does not immediately interpret the identity of these two olive trees/branches. Instead, the word of the Lord was this: "Not by might nor by power, but by my Spirit, says the LORD Almighty" (v. 6). God's word for Zerubbabel was that any work he or any of the returnees from the exile in Babylon was going to do would only be accomplished by the power of the Spirit of God. Reliance on human resources, sagacity or strength would be fruitless. Yes, the Temple had to be rebuilt, but it would never be accomplished by the dint of human force. Zerubbabel and the returnees needed the supply of "oil" that comes from the Holy Spirit, or they would burn themselves out needlessly. Thus, what the "golden oil" (v. 12b) was to the fluted lamps so the Holy Spirit would be for all who would depend on him to complete the rebuilding of the Temple.

God's Work Must Not Be Despised for Its Small Beginnings – 4:7–10

The Lord immediately applies the principle of verse 6 in verse 7. The "mighty mountain" surely is a metaphorical allusion to some of the obstacles or difficulties that must have presented themselves in the building of the Temple to Zerubbabel. But all such obstacles that seemed at the moment as mountains would be flattened out and "become as level ground" (v 7). Ezra 4:1–4 and 5:3–5 pointed to some such obstacles, but if now the work would be carried out according to the principle announced in verse 6, then all would go much more smoothly.

The reference to the "capstone" in verse 7 probably pointed to the fact that the Temple would soon be completed. This could not be a reference to a foundation stone, for it had been laid many years ago (Ezra 3:1–10). But this was the stone of "topping out" the whole project. The shouts that would accompany it represented the culminating act where the people together would shout praises to God for his favor in aiding them to complete the task.

Lesson 6

Purging the Wicked from Israel
Zechariah 5:1–4

Visions six and seven again are twin messages in the chiastic arrangement of the eight night-visions. These two are linked by their concern over wickedness. In the sixth vision (vv. 1–4), wickedness is removed from Israel, but in the seventh (vv. 5–11), the very principle of wickedness and evil are removed from the whole earth. Vision six, with its removal of wickedness from Jerusalem, is related to vision three, which describes a new Jerusalem where the Lord dwells. Again, in vision seven, where evil itself is removed from Jerusalem to the land of Babylon, it parallels vision two, where God will remove the horns that have been raised up against Jerusalem by the craftsmen he has appointed.

With so much evil, wickedness and sin in Israel, one might begin to think that it would be enough to cancel out any blessing that might come on the people of God from the rebuilding of the Temple. To put the question in this way is reminiscent of the point made by Zechariah's colleague, the prophet Haggai. He had asked the priests in Haggai 2:12–13 if holiness was indeed "catchy, " i.e., transferable just by contact. Of course, it was not. Sin was much more easily communicated, but holiness did not operate on the same basis. Therefore, in this situation, one work of obedience in building the Temple of God was not enough to offset the people's need for holiness in every aspect of their living!

In this sixth vision, theft and lying under oath are the crimes the Lord focused on. This is because theft was both at the center of the second table of the Decalogue and it symbolizes the lack of love for our neighbor while perjury was at the center of the first table of the Ten Commandments and points to our denial of our Lord God.

The Evil of the Wicked Unfurled – 5:1–2

As the prophet looked, he saw a "flying scroll" (5:1) twenty cubits long and ten cubits wide, or about 30 feet long and 15 feet wide. The Hebrew word used is *megillah*, "roll, scroll." This scroll that the prophet was shown must have been open or spread out so it could be read on what was written on it on both sides (v. 3b).

Commentators point to a strikingly parallel passage in Ezekiel 2:9–10.

Then I looked, and I saw a hand stretched out to me. In it was a scroll, which was unrolled before me. On both sides of it were written words of lament and mourning and woe.

What was written on the scroll Zechariah saw involved a "curse" (Hebrew *ha-alah*) that involved the whole land of Israel. This made it like the scroll Ezekiel saw, for his had words of "lament, mourning, and woes." Ezekiel's list of sad words may have been the curses that Moses had warned would come on Israel (Deut. 28:15–68) if they insisted on departing from the Lord. In fact, Ezekiel 30:1 refers to all of these curses in the singular as "the curse."

It is true, of course, that only two transgressions of the law are specified here in this vision: theft and perjury. But these two are samples and ways of briefly summarizing the whole of the Decalogue.

But why were the scroll's dimensions so carefully noted? Before bound books appeared, scrolls were the means of recording writing. These were long pieces of papyrus or parchment, some extending 30 to 60 feet long.

But why was this scroll so wide? The text gives no special reason for the dimensions; nevertheless, interpreters have noted that these are the same dimensions for the Holy Place in the Tabernacle (Ex. 26:15–28) and for the porch of the Temple (1 Kgs. 6:3). From these observations, interpreters have inferred that judgment must begin at the house of God with the people of God before others outside the believing community are judged.

These interpreters may have drawn inference from the size of the scroll. Judgment would indeed begin at the house of God, for key parts of the Tabernacle and Temple shared the same dimensions. Moreover, the fact that the scroll was "flying" likened the message to the advertisements one can often see at the ocean seashores. Small aircrafts fly low over the beaches, with long trailing banners flying behind them to attract people to certain stores. But in this case, the message was from God himself and it involved pending judgment.

The Evil of the Wicked Condemned – 5:3–4

The message of the flying scroll was that there was a "curse" that was "going out over the whole land" (or "the whole earth") (3a). The reason for this curse could be summarized in two types of evildoers. These two classes of evil doers violated the injunctions of both tables of the Law of God. Exodus 20:15 had warned against sinning against our neighbor:

"You shall not steal." Exodus 20:7 had warned about sinning against the Lord God: "You shall not take the name of the LORD your God in vain."

Stealing violated the possessions that belonged to another person, which in turn showed disrespect for the whole second table of the law. Instead of favoring each other with acts of love, this violation of thievery did the exact opposite; it showed disregard not only for persons, but for God who has warned this was not to be done.

Perjury violated the very person, name and character of God. His name was to be used cautiously, not flippantly. Nor was his name to be used thoughtlessly or for no purpose, as some do in praying extemporaneously with the frequent interjection of God's name that served no grammatical (or any other) purpose for where it was constantly being interjected. Both of these commands were taken from the middle of each of the two tables of the law, which might strengthen the idea that the whole Decalogue was being inferred by so doing.

Verse 4 introduces one of the most solemn texts in the Bible, for it warned that God would "send [the curse] out" and "it [would] enter the house of the thief and the house of anyone who [swore] falsely by [his] name." Nothing was more certain than the fact that God's judgments would overtake the wicked. They would not escape the punishment that was due them. That curse would "enter the house" of those who practiced evil; these perpetrators of evil could not hide even in their own homes where they thought God might be able to escape from his punishment. Moreover, not only was that punishment sure and certain, but it also would be permanent, for it would "remain/abide" "in that house." (v. 4b). The Hebrew word for "remain/abide" is *laneh* from *lun*, "to spend the night," or "to lodge." The curse of God, then, would stay in that house day and night to do its work of judgment for which it would be sent.

But even more damaging is the final clause in verse 4c: It would "consume/destroy [that house] completely, both its timbers and its stones." What a climax to sin and repeated calls to ask God for his forgiveness. The only escape would be to be cleansed of such sin by the pardoning grace of our Lord Yeshua. Only he could remove the curse of the law, for he became a curse in our place (Gal. 3:13).

Conclusions

1. God's people gave praise to the Lord when the Temple was completed, but such a fine piece of work could not be an excuse for their tolerating evil in their midst in other areas of their lives.

2. Using God's name falsely, or for no purpose, was a violation of his person and character. Perjurers would face the wrath of God. How then can we tolerate Hollywood's films with their awful profanity and vile use of God's name repeatedly in her films?

3. Stealing what belonged to others was a violation of God's warning not to do so in any shape of manner. It was a slur against God for what he had or had not given to us and therefore it led us to take from others what was theirs.

4. God will send out his judgment on all perpetrators of evil in a form that will show it is certain and permanent.

Lesson 7

Removing Wickedness from Israel
Zechariah 5:5–11

The angel who had been interpreting these visions for the prophet seems to have withdrawn, perhaps to allow the prophet time to reflect on all that the flying scroll meant. But then this angel "came forward," urging the prophet to "Look up and see what [was] appearing" (v. 5).

In this seventh vision, sin and wickedness were to be totally removed from the land of Judah to the land of Babylon. Since "wickedness" is a feminine word, it is here symbolized as a woman, who is thrust into an ephah, sealed with a lead cover over the top and carried by two women into the ancient land of Shinar (modern-day Iraq).

Wickedness Will Be Placed Under Wraps – 5:5–8

Zechariah was shown a "basket" (v. 6), or "ephah." This container for dry goods is difficult to describe exactly, for it held somewhere between 3/8 and 2/3 of a bushel. If those measurements are correct, this was too small for a woman to fit into it. But such an objection does not impinge on interpreting apocalyptic literature, especially where it involves dreams and visions, for there is not in this literature the usual concern to depict reality directly. Anyway, it merely uses the figure of a woman to depict "wickedness."

If we seek what this new principle or power was that formed such an influence over the Jewish people, the answer was commerce or trade, as indicated by the ephah, its natural symbol. Thus, during the days of Israel's exile, she was transformed from being an agricultural and pastoral people into a nation of merchants. Also, along with the ephah, we have the "cover" (Hebrew *kikar*, "circle"; some interpret it "talent"). Nowhere else is this word rendered "cover," but it is always a fixed weight by which silver, gold and other things are measured. Thus the "talent" or circular mass of lead was what had kept the woman (the "wickedness") under cover, so to speak.

The angel quickly added, "This [woman] is the iniquity of the people throughout the land" (v. 6c). Wickedness stood for everything that was the opposite of righteousness—whether it was in the ethical, moral, civil or religious realm—but especially commercial types of cheating. That, then, was what this woman represented here. This was not a picture of a genie in a jar, but it was wickedness and evil that was apparently connected with mercantile commercialism, for which the country of Babylon had a reputation both in ancient and now in modern times, which now seemed to be uniquely fitted for such a dubious title especially because of its oil cartel in our day. Commerce increasingly brought the nations of the world under its sway, for legislation and government began to accommodate themselves to the demands of commercialism.

This woman's influence depicting wickedness was capped by a "cover/circle of lead" (v. 7). Thus, it was God alone who had kept wickedness concealed. Even though wickedness had grown large (perhaps by the bushel full), it would no longer prevail against God himself. One of God's great acts in history would be the removing of the wicked (vision 6) as well as removing wickedness itself (vision 7). Revelation 18 describes a similar closing scene in world history as the Lord deals with the merchants who are there called "the great men of the earth" and the key commercial city is regarded as "queen of the nations."

Housed in Babylon – 5:9–11

Suddenly the prophet saw two women coming with "the wind in their wings" (v. 9b). Their wings were "like those of a stork" (9c). The Hebrew word for "stork" is *hasida*, "fruitful one." Whether that is why the "stork" is invoked here as a symbol of God's gracious removal of sin and iniquity from his people in like manner of his removing the sin of dung-spattered Joshua (Zech. 3:4), or because of the enormous wing span of the storks who can fly for hours on end as they migrate, cannot be determined here.

The woman in the ephah will be transferred to "the land of Shinar/Babylon" (v. 11). Shinar was the ancient name for that part of Babylon that contained the cities of Babel (Babylon), Erech, Accad and Calneh (Gen. 10:10; 11:2; Dan. 1:2). It was in this land where God would build a house for wickedness (v. 11). Thus, evil and unrighteousness would be far removed from the people of God. What began as the Tower of Babel (Gen. 11) would become the site for the ephah that would be set there on its base (v. 11c).

Babylon, of course, plays a major part in the eschatological drama of the closing days of world history. Isaiah 13–14 and Jeremiah 50–51 place a revived Babylonian empire at the center of the final contest between God and "all the nations of the earth." God will triumph, for he is fully in control as can be seen from his ability to pack up evil and ship it off to where the center of wickedness will make its final stand. There God will deal conclusively with evil.

Conclusions

1. Commerce and commercialism are not intrinsically evil. But if commerce begins to dominate men and nations and it starts influencing the way governments and business operates, then evil has captured the means of production and the heart of a nation.

2. Women are not to be regarded as instruments of evil and wickedness.

3. All who follow the ways of wickedness will be overtaken by sin and evil.

4. The best way to deal with evil is to call upon God to remove it altogether.

5. God is able in the meantime to put a lid on evil before he finally removes it once and for all to the center of wickedness.

6. Shinar/Babylon is a world power that is so antagonistic to God that it represents all that opposes him.

Lesson 8

Executing Judgment on the
Gentile Nations and Crowning Joshua
Zechariah 6:1–15

The eighth and final night-vision corresponds to the first vision, for both concern Israel's relation to the Gentile nations. But whereas the first vision ended with the disappointing news from the equestrian patrol that all the Gentile nations were at rest, the eighth vision had war chariots attached to the four horses so that they could dispense the threatened judgment and carried a pleasing message that justice had been meted out.

In this lesson, we also cover the crowning of Joshua the High Priest along with its inclusion of another message concerning Messiah as the "Branch" (6:9–14). The passages ends, therefore with verse 15, which returns to the building of the Temple, only this one will be built by men who come from "far away": Gentiles coming from the ends of the earth.

By Appeasing God's Wrath Against the Gentile Nations – 6:1–8

The mission and the tasks of the horses and chariots appears to be the dominant theme of all the visions, as they appear in the first and last night-visions and act as bookends that embrace the start and the completion of all eight. As a total, the eight visions amount to more than the simple insistence that the Temple of the Lord must be rebuilt, or the leadership revived; they argue for the renewal of God's kingdom in the whole world and for the fact that those governments that opposed Messiah's kingdom must and will be totally vanquished. But the kingdom of Messiah will never be destroyed!

As the interpreting angel no doubt directs the prophet again, he lifts his eyes in time to see four chariots going forth from "two mountains—mountains of bronze" (6:1). This vision was not just about four horses as seen in the first vision, but they were hitched up to "four chariots," which appear to be war chariots. Their purpose was to dispense judgment. The horses were of various colors: the first chariot was drawn by "red" horses, the second by "black" horses, the third by "white" horses, and the fourth by "dappled/speckled/pale" horses (vv. 2–3). So, what is their meaning?

Whereas the horses in the first vision came up from a "hollow/valley" (1:8), the four chariots here come from the "two mountains—mountains of bronze" (6:1). These are never identified by the angel, nor does the prophet ask what they mean and why they are of "bronze." However, it is quite common to see modern interpreters identify these two mountains as Mount Zion and the Mount of Olives. Others agree, but they also note that the Valley of Jehoshaphat (meaning "ADONAI will judge") is located in between these mountains, the apparent place where God will judge the nations (Joel 3:2).

But the question remains: Why are these mountains made of bronze? Are the "bronze mountains" just part of the apocalyptic drapery and serve merely to let us know that the vision is supernatural in its setting? Or does the "bronze" point to the strength and sublimity of the power of God that is over this whole operation? It does not seem possible to say what is the correct interpretation.

Let's look more closely at the "chariots." Zechariah asked what they meant (v. 4). The answer came in v. 5: "These are the four spirits of heaven, going out from standing in the presence of the Lord of the whole earth." The verb "going out" is frequently used in the last three visions, occurring some twelve times. It is often used of the king and his army going out on a military mission; if so, then the whole world is being prepared for God's concluding act in history. God restores Israel to her land and assumes the reign of the world.

Why does the text identify four chariots but pass over the first one, with the "red" horses, in this explanation? The "black" horses are sent forth to the "north country"; the "dappled" ones are sent to the "south" (v. 6). Some translators send the "white" horses to the "west," but the Hebrew text merely has the white horses being sent "after them," i.e., after the black horses. Does this mean the white horses and chariots were also sent to the north country, or does it refer to what it was "after" or in "back" or behind them (the Israelite orientation was always to the east, so the "west" was in back of them), meaning the "west"? The "red" team seems to be held in reserve as the other three teams are sent on a mission.

So, what are the "four winds/spirits of heaven" meant to signify (v. 5)? These may be the same "four winds" Daniel referred to in Daniel 7:1–3 that brought forth the four great Gentile world-powers. Here, however, the four winds break up the empires as one world power after another rises, only to fall from its position of eminence. They are the Babylonian empire, the Medo-Persian, the Greco-Macedonian and the Roman or Western empires.

What about the meaning of the colors of the horses? The colors figure prominently in this vision, and the horses bear a strong resemblance to the "four horsemen" of Revelation 6:1–8, where "red" stood for martyrdom, "white" for victory, "black" for famine, and the "dappled or pale" horseman stood for a mixture that indicated death. Could that also be part of their function here?

The first of the great world-powers was the Babylonian Empire, which had already oppressed Israel and had laid waste to Jerusalem in 586 BCE That was one of the north countries. This empire's destruction of its rule and reign in 539 BCE was followed by the work of the black war chariot, closely followed by the white war chariot, as they would also take out other northern countries in days to come: Medo-Persia and the Greco-Macedonian countries.

While these war chariots went north, the dappled or speckled horses went south, presumably to the country of Egypt, as Daniel 11 identifies the south country. It could also be that they went even to the African countries.

Verse 7 exhibits a strong contrast with the report the horsemen give in 1:11, where "the whole world is at rest and in peace." In this vision, however, the "powerful horses" now do their work appeasing the wrath of God. Thus, King Cyrus' Medo-Persian victory over Babylon in 539 BCE was the first of a series of victories that would come.

The steeds in v. 7 are described as being "strong" or "powerful" as they do their work of appeasing God's wrath (v. 8). Others tend to link the aspect of "strength" as the outstanding feature of the fourth steed, connecting it to the need for strength to meet the challenge in the parallel passage in Daniel 7:7, where Daniel's fourth beast that came up out of the sea was "exceedingly strong" and had "great iron teeth" that "devoured and broke in pieces" everything. It represented that fourth kingdom as one that stamped on everything with its feet and had ten horns on its head. But set against such might from the hand of mere mortals is the overwhelming power of God, who will be more than a match for all such human shows of force and might.

Verse 8 concludes this first section with an assurance that those who have gone out to the north countries have been effective and brought "rest" to our Lord. While Cyrus' victory over Babylon in 539 was only the first of the promised victories God would win, it is apparently only when Babylon falls in the final day that God's Spirit (Hebrew, *Ruach*) will rest, after he has won complete vindication for the persecuted people of Israel.

By Installing God's Priest-King as Ruler Over All Nations – 6:9–15

The concluding and climactic act of the eight night visions is now described in verses 9–15, in which the High Priest Joshua is crowned as a representative of Messiah who is to come. This act, however, does not take place in a vision as the previous eight revelations had occurred, but it is an act that is placed in the midst of the people. Zechariah will indeed receive a delegation of three men, who had arrived from Babylon bearing the special gift of "silver and gold." This presentation follows the banishment of evil from the land and the destruction of all human world empires and political powers, which now allows for the crowning of the true and real king over the whole earth—Yeshua the Messiah.

Three men named Heldai, Tobijah, and Jedaiah, who apparently are recent returnees from the exile in Babylon, carry such a gift from those still in exile. Zechariah was to go at once ("on the same day") to the "house of Josiah, son of Zephaniah," who is otherwise unknown to us, but it seemed he was one who was given to hospitality. Could this then mean that the Spirit of God was opening the prophet's spiritual understanding to be ready for a future day in which even the Gentile peoples from "far away/far off" (v. 15) would come and bring their gifts to the house of God as acts of worship and thanksgiving to the Lord?

Zechariah was told to "take the silver and the gold and make a crown and set it on the head of the High Priest, Joshua, son of Jozadak" (v. 11). The word for crown is in the plural number in the Hebrew text, which has led some commentators to argue that there were two crowns: one for the High Priest and one for royalty. But this does not agree with what follows, for the prophet was to take the newly formed crown and put it on the head of Joshua, the High Priest. Thus, the plural number refers to a single crown that is splendid and magnificent in its own rights—a plurality of majesty!

This coronation ceremony of Joshua introduced five magnificent Messianic prophecies that form one of the grandest moments in biblical revelation. Zechariah was to announce these momentous declarations:

1. "Behold the man whose name is the Branch" (v. 12b). This arousing announcement reminds us of the charge given to the prophet Isaiah in 40:9, "Say unto the cities of Judah, Behold your God" or 52:13, "Behold my Servant," who was no less than Yeshua. But in this case, the word "Behold" called attention to the second person of the Trinity, Messiah, who had three times previously been addressed as "Branch" ("the Branch," "a king who shall reign," Jer. 23:3–5; "My Servant the Branch," Zech. 3:8; "the Branch of the LORD," Isa. 4:2). And now the "Man whose name is the Branch." Of course, Joshua could never wear the crown or rule upon a throne, but God had promised that he would unite the two great mediatory offices of

Priest and King into one person in Psalm 110:4–6 – for he had promised to Messiah, "You are a priest forever … [you] will crush kings on the day of [your] wrath… [You] will judge the nations."

2. "He will branch out from his place" (v. 12c). Even though for a while it seemed as if Messiah was no more than "a root out of the dry and parched ground" (Isa. 53:2), yet God would prosper him and elevate him above all principalities and powers as he "branched out" (2 Sam. 23:1; Ps. 89:19). He had begun as the "Seed" of Abraham, then he sprouted from the scepter of the tribe of Judah, and even further still, he emerged from the line of David, and further developed on the soil of Judah in Bethlehem-Ephrata as a baby, where later he walked the shores of the Sea of Galilee, teaching and healing the lost and the sick.

3. He himself will "build the Temple of the LORD" (v. 12d). The repeated emphasis given to the pronoun "he" was to make sure the certainty and greatness of the task of rebuilding the Temple was clearly seen. True, Zerubbabel, the governor, under the preaching of Haggai and Zechariah, had built what we now call the "Second Temple" in 515 BCE, which stood until 70 CE, yet Messiah would build a third new Temple in the coming new age (Isa. 2:2–4; Ezek. 40–42; Mic. 4:1–5; Hag. 2:7–9). Once again, the pronoun "he" is emphasized by its repetition in v. 13b, as he himself is declared to be "clothed with majesty" or regal glory as no one else has ever borne it (Ps. 96:6).

4. He "will sit and rule on his throne" (v. 13c). Therefore, all authority and all rule would be exercised by Messiah's royal power. This power and authority had been promised long ago to the scion of David, who, unlike all the former line of monarchs in the empires of men, saw their kingdoms destroyed and overthrown. But here was a throne that would last "forever" (2 Sam. 7:12–16). All power and all authority in heaven and earth would one day belong to Messiah, who would sit on the throne of David as king and Lord forever and ever: "He will be a priest on his throne. And there will be harmony between the two," i.e., between the office of priest and Davidic king (13 d, e; Ps. 110:4–5; Heb. 7).

Thus, Zechariah daringly combines the priestly and kingly offices in one person, the Messiah, also called the "Branch." Only Yeshua can deal with the sin of Judah (as priest) and the world (as king) "in one day" and yet also remove all tensions between political and racial issues remaining from the ages. In Messiah there is perfect harmony, for the will of the Father and the Son is one, and so harmony and peace can come on the nations after he has judged them in his wrath!

The crown would be deposited in the Temple of God as a "memorial," not only as a reminder of the three distinguished strangers who had brought this gift from the exiles, but also as an act of kindness from those who were "far away" (v. 15a) and symbolic of what would take place in the later days of the end times. This expression, "far away/far off," was a circumlocution for referring to the "Gentiles" as seen in Acts 2:39 or Ephesians 2:13. The full realization waits until Messiah sits and reigns as priest on his throne over Israel and the world.

This prophecy ends in v. 15c: "This will happen if you diligently obey the LORD your God." The fulfillment of this prophecy is not conditioned on their obedience; this promise rests on the unchangeable purpose and will of God alone. But the aspect of their *participation* in this promise does rest on their obedience. This phrase is taken from Deuteronomy 28:1. Thus, all the promises of the old covenant would be enjoyed only if they are participated in by a faith that obeyed and did what the Lord said. If they felt they had no power to hearken diligently to all God has said, they could apply for the grace of God, who would give them one heart and one way to fear him forever (Jer. 32:38–41).

Conclusions

1. God would rouse his horsemen and chariots to vindicate his wrath on those nations that had perpetually resisted his grace and mercy and despised his law.

2. God's "Branch," the Messiah, would have the dual role of being both priest and king even as Psalm 110 had promised in the type of Melchizedek.

3. This "Branch" of God would "branch out" from his roots that seemed unattractive at first but would climax in a triumph heard round the cosmos.

4. Messiah would build a new future Temple that would bear his glory and honor.

5. Messiah would sit and rule forever on the throne of David over the whole universe and over all men and women.

Lesson 9

What It Means to Be the People of God: Then and Now
Zechariah 7:1–8:23

We now come to the third main block of text in the four sections of Zechariah's prophecies as it is now presented in chapters 7–8. Some commentators regard some portions of this unit, such as Zechariah 7:7–10, as one of the finest summaries of the teachings of the former prophets.

Almost two years had passed since the night of the eight visions, in which God's future plans for Israel and the nations had been set out. Accordingly, on the fourth day of the ninth month (our month of December), known on their calendar as Kislev, in the fourth year of King Darius' reign, this new word came from God. This prophecy came in four distinct segments, each introduced by the expression: "Then the word of the LORD Almighty came to me" (7:4, 8; 8:1, 18).

The fourth year of King Darius was a good year. Things were going well and seemed promising for the exiles who had returned from Babylon. Darius had issued his royal decree removing all hindrances for Judah's rebuilding of the Temple in Jerusalem (Ezra 6). From Haggai 1:4, it would seem that even some of the homes that had stood in ruins in Jerusalem were now being rebuilt, along with portions of the wall around the city. But there still was a note of uneasiness despite these good signs. For example, a delegation of two men were sent from Bethel to inquire if the city's people should continue to weep and fast in the fifth month, commemorating the destruction of the city of Jerusalem, as they had been doing for years. This was most interesting, for the Jewish people from the ten northern tribes had deputized Sharezer, whose full name must have been Nergal-Shar-Ezer ("may Nergal protect the king") and Regem-Meleck ("friend of the king"), to go and inquire from the priests down in Jerusalem if they should continue to observe the fast they had noted each year on that date? It may be that these Jewish men had Babylonian names bestowed on them by those who now ruled them, just as Daniel and his three friends had when they were taken captive from Judah by the Babylonians (Dan. 1).

Interestingly, this delegation was sent from Bethel in northern Israel to those segregated brethren down south to inquire about a religious question. When Joshua had originally divided up the land among the twelve tribes of Israel, Bethel had been given to the tribe of Benjamin (Josh. 18:13). But when the northern ten tribes broke away from the house of David under Jeroboam's leadership, Bethel somehow was made that part of Benjamin sided with the northern tribes. So it became the center for the worship of one of the two bull calves that were set up as religious substitutes for those who previously had been in the habit of going to Jerusalem's Temple to worship God in Judah. Thus, the fact that the delegation now came from this city of the false idolatrous bull-calf worship in Bethel should not be lost on anyone trying to understand what was going on in this surprising change of events. It could well be that the lessons of Assyrian conquest of Samaria (721 BCE) and the Babylonian captivities (606, 598, 586) had forced the populace in Bethel to not look for any hope or relief from the northern confederation of tribes or from their idolatrous center of worship. It was time to seek the Lord God at his Temple in Jerusalem!

These two men entreated the favor of the Lord and asked the priests of the Lord God in the south about whether they should continue to fast in the fifth month. In fact, Moses had taught that it was indeed the priests who were to teach the people (Deut. 33:8–10; later Mal. 2:5–7). Therefore, this is why the delegation turned to the priests of ADONAI in Jerusalem as the proper source to obtain an answer.

Are We Serving Ourselves or God? – 7:1–7

This delegation came to Jerusalem and began their mission by entreating the favor of ADONAI with the presentation of gifts and offerings (v. 2). They then addressed their question to the priests in the House of the Lord, as Moses had taught they should.

Their question was, "Should I [the city of Bethel and the people up north] mourn and fast in the fifth month, as I have done for sin for so many years?" (v. 2c). The "fast" they wanted to know about was the one that came in the "fifth month," the 9th day of Ab, or our month of August. This date memorialized the day Nebuchadnezzar destroyed Jerusalem. But Jewish historians and the Talmud added a longer list of calamities that took place about this date. For the delegation, their request only had reference to the destruction of the First Temple by the Babylonians in 586. This fuller list included both some earlier and later events:

1. The day God decreed the people would not enter the promised land because of their unbelief was set, but instead they would wander in the wilderness until that generation had died.

2. On this very same day not only was the First Temple destroyed, but the Second Temple was destroyed later in 70 CE by the Romans.

3. On this same day, the city of Bethar in Israel was taken from under the false messiah named Bar Kochba.

4. On this day, Bar Kochba was captured and put to death because of his improper claim to be the Messiah.

5. On this day, the wicked Turnus Rufus ploughed up the hill where the Temple stood, thus fulfilling Micah's prophecy that "Zion shall be plowed as a field" (3:12).

The answer to their request would be given in two major parts, one negative (7:4–14) and the other positive (8:1–23). These responses were further divided into two subsections, each beginning with the introductory formula of "Then the word of the LORD Almighty came to me" (7:4, 8; 8:1, 18).

These four messages are introduced first by a call to repentance and the sad reminder that all their troubles had come upon them because of their disobedience to the word God had given them through his prophets. Thus, this section begins in 7:4–14 much as the introductory message had in 1:1–6.

When the Lord answered through the prophet, he did not speak only to the delegation but addressed his words to "all the people of the land" (v. 5a). He also began with a question: "When you fasted and mourned in the fifth and seventh months for the past seventy years, was it really for me that you fasted?" (v. 5b). God knew the question showed that Israel had the false idea that abstaining from food and water was itself meritorious. But even this ritual focused on themselves and not on the Living God. Such mourning and abstaining were not for those who were practicing it as an external sign of an inward sorrow or of repentance for their sin. Instead, it was grief and disappointment over the tragedy and calamity that had befallen them. More, as God had not ordained such fasts to be held on the fifth or seventh months, these rituals were self-designed and self-imposed. These events were tokens of self-glorification, focused on themselves and not on the Lord who was over all history. Therefore, these fasts were self-condemning, for they were done with complete indifference to what God had called them to do; they did only what they thought was good and right.

Believers are taught in 1 Corinthians 10:31 that whether they eat or drink, or whatever they do, they are to do all of it to the glory of God. That is why v. 7 ends with another question God had for Israel: "Are these not words the LORD proclaimed through the earlier prophets when Jerusalem and its surrounding towns were at rest and prosperous?" All this was not brand-new teaching; this same Israel had already been through such times as these often in the past. Those were better days in that there still was time to repent because of the very goodness of God to them; that time had now expired!

Instead, the Israelites offered to God outward acts of religiosity, more fasting in place of true and sorrowful repentance. In fact, the prophet Isaiah recalled in chapter 58 that the people even remonstrated with God saying, "Why have we fasted and you haven't taken notice at all?" But the Lord pronounced such days of fasting as days in which they found their own pleasures above the sober act of real repentance. They all erred in thinking that God had great delight in their sacrifices per se; rather, what the Lord wanted was persons who would obey his voice and follow him (1 Sam. 15:22–23). That is what God required: "justice, mercy and walking humbly with one's God" (Mic. 6:6–8).

So, who are we and Israel serving—ourselves or the Lord? Ritual, order, service and worship may be wasted energy that has no effect in the spiritual realm, because our work is not by might, nor by power, nor is it by God's Spirit, but it is solely by our own wills.

Are We Listening to Ourselves or God? – 7:8–14

As noted, this section is very reminiscent of Isaiah 58:6–12, recalling its substance. The emphasis was on each person's duty toward their neighbors and those in need as tantamount to duty to God. He expects that "justice" will always be administered for those needing to be defended. He also expects mercy and compassion to be the hallmark of our responses to our fellow human beings as actions that are consistent with our love for him. We are never to take advantage of the widow, the orphan, the foreigner, nor the poor. Further, there was to be no plotting of evil against each other (7:9–10).

Believers may maliciously and incorrectly tend to think these are merely warnings from the Law of Moses for the people of Israel and that Gentile believers are now free from the law because we are under the Law of Messiah. Or there may be an attempt to pass this off as a form of obedience to the word of God as nothing more than the "social gospel." Both objections are roadblocks we sometimes raise to following God's inscribed will. Even in the New Testament, we have a debt of love we owe to all men. There we are also commanded to live and act righteously and justly before all mortals. The same Lord still expects the same kind of response from all his followers.

Tragically, the result of this divine call to listen to the voice of God in these matters resulted then in that day (as it often does in our day) in the outright rejection of any obedience that God laid out for his people (7:11–12). They just refused to listen to what God said through his prophet, and they showed contempt through their body language, pulling their shoulder away and stopping up their ears. They made their hearts "as hard as flint" (v. 12a; cf. Ezek. 3:9; Jer. 17:1), which invited the wrath of God to fall on them. It did not matter that God had sent his servants the prophets to teach them and his Holy Spirit to help them understand. They just did not want any parts of anything God had to say to them! No wonder Zechariah had urged, "Do not be as your fathers, to whom the former prophets cried, saying: 'Turn now from your evil ways and your evil doings'" (1:4–6).

God kept calling to the nation of Israel, but they paid no attention. That is why he scattered that nation by a whirlwind all over the globe (v. 13). Also, the land of Israel would be left desolate in their absence so that few travelers passed through it (v. 14). In fact, the last words of the Hebrew Bible, which ends with 2 Chronicles 36:14–16, leaves us with these mournful declarations:

> Furthermore, all the leaders of the priests and the people became more and more unfaithful, following all the detestable practices of the nations and defiling the Temple of the LORD, which he had consecrated in Jerusalem. The LORD, the God of their ancestors, sent word to them through his messengers again and again, because he had pity on the people and on his dwelling place. But they mocked God's messengers, despised his words, and scoffed at his prophets until the wrath of God was aroused against this people and there was no remedy.

Are We Believing a Lie or the Truth? – 8:1–17

Despite the bad memories of Israel's past deeds of disobedience, God will go beyond such painful realities to paint a bright picture of the future. The sub-themes of this passage provide us with a potpourri of topics taken from Zechariah's messages over the years, as indicated by the ten occurrences of the formula: "This is what the LORD Almighty says" (8:2, 3, 4, 6, 7, 9, 20, 23). Each of these sub-themes raised an appropriate question for that day and for ours. It is clear that the authority of the Lord is what authenticates the message that Zechariah announces, for that is what the introductory formula for each segment announced repeatedly.

A. Do we believe God's zeal for his promise to Israel, and his hot anger against the nations that oppress Israel, still controls the facts of life? (8:2)

Because the Lord's love for Israel, his jealousy is stirred so that its heat is raised against the nations that oppressed her. He was just "a little displeased" with Israel when he handed them over to their enemies (Jer. 12:7), but the enemies showed no mercy and went way beyond what God had intended for them to do against these enemies.

God's zeal or jealousy must be understood in this context, for if it is likened to human jealousy, it will conjure up concepts such as Aristotle taught, i.e., that jealousy is a way of mortals "getting even" with a person who has hurt them. But in our Lord, "zeal" or "jealousy" is the stirring of the emotions of his soul so that he wants to see right, justice and fairness vindicated, but there is no need in the divine person to "get even" or retaliate to even up the score. How could anything, or anyone, be "even" with God? There is no green-eyed monster that has the Lord God wanting to get back at someone for what they have done to him or against him. Instead, our Lord was zealous for his covenant that he had made with the patriarchs and David; he would be faithful to what he had promised.

B. Do we believe God will return to dwell in Jerusalem? (8:3)

Two verbs dominate this section: "I will return to Zion" and "[I will] dwell in Jerusalem." The word for "return" takes us back to 1:16, and the word to "dwell" to 2:10. This signifies that God will restore his favor and blessing toward Israel once more in that future day. Such a promise can be fulfilled only by Messiah's second return and his visibly ruling and reigning from Mount Zion amid a restored and converted Israel. It is sad to see some commentators conclude that this promised return and dwelling of God with his people signifies nothing more than the restoring of favor to the people of God. This is too minimal an interpretation. Moreover, since Ezekiel saw the slow departure of the glory of the Lord from the Temple and Jerusalem, this text has the return and promise of God's dwelling once more in our midst (also in Hos. 5:15; 6:1–3).

Jerusalem will be called the "city of truth" and the "mountain of the LORD Almighty will be called the Holy Mountain" (v. 3). That is because Jerusalem will be the seat where the true and faithful God dwells, and it will be "holy" because he has taken up his abode there once again. Moreover, there will be no will to do iniquity there or any speaking of lies (Zeph. 3:13).

C. *Do we believe Jerusalem will be repopulated? (8:4–5)*

Old men and women, along with boys and girls, will be able to live in Jerusalem without fear of being victimized or attacked by a criminal or an invader or even of being mugged by a predator. This is a future time when peace and security can be realized as the new norm. This is a picture of the rule and reign of Messiah on earth, and he will be centered in Jerusalem. It is clear, however, that there still is another question.

D. *Do we believe it is too difficult for God to bring back a full remnant of his people? (8:6)*

The verb repeated twice in v. 6 is "to be marvelous" (Hebrew *pale`*, "to be wonderful," "to be marvelous," "to [do what is] hard," "to [do what is] difficult"). This same word appears in Genesis 18:14, where Sarah is asked a similar question by our Lord, after being told she shall bear a son when she is 90 years old. The question is: "Is anything too hard/marvelous for the LORD?" This word that also appears twice in the chapter in Jeremiah is very much like the contents of Zechariah 8. Jeremiah also asks, when he is told to purchase some real estate just as the Babylonian conqueror is at the gates of Jerusalem: "Is anything too hard/wonderful for the LORD?" (Jer. 32: 17; repeated by the Lord in 32:27).

Therefore, the question remains: Why do we think that restoring Israel back to her land is something just too difficult and too miraculous to even consider? But that is exactly what God is doing right now: some 6 1/2 million Jews have returned to the land of Israel: an amount that may approximate almost one half of all Jewish people in the world!

E. *Do we believe a restored remnant will come from all over the world? (8:7–8)*

These two verses make up one of the greatest, most comprehensive promises of Israel's restoration and conversion. The restoration will come from all parts of the earth, or as Zechariah said, "from the land of the rising of the sun and from the land of the going down of the sun." Such a restoration could hardly represent the few who came back from the Babylonian captivity. More, this return came only from one direction, the north, if we count the avoidance of the desert, which was directly in the path of those traveling from the east. This promise of a return from all over the world is like the one in Isaiah 11:11–12 and 43:5–6. Such a promise of such a massive restoration of Israel was a demonstration of the greatness of God's mercy and faithfulness to his word. God would betroth Israel to himself as his wife once again (Hos. 2:19–20). This is exactly what Jeremiah 32:38–41 had also promised.

F. Do we believe God will give the increase? (8:9–13)

The encouragement from the Lord in v. 9 was the same word Haggai gave in 2:4: "Let your hands be strong." Those words had been used on more than one occasion, for we find them used as an exhortation for those going into battle in Israel (Judg. 7:11; 2 Sam. 2:7; 16:21). In this context, it was used by the prophets who spoke in the day the foundation was laid for the house of the Lord (v. 9).

Again, like Haggai 1:6, the Lord contrasts conditions prior to the days before the word of the Lord came and conditions as they existed now that that word from the Lord had been heard (v. 11). The repentance of the people had also provided the grounds for our Lord to reverse the adverse conditions of this struggling small community of exiles.

Not only were the general conditions changed, but so was the condition of the soil, as reported in Haggai 2:19. Repentance and a national revival had produced a change in the productivity of the ground. Thus, the connection between the sin of mortals and the curse on the ground was reversed by the word of God and the repentance of the people!

Zechariah 8:13 traces one more contrast between the past and the present. While in the past Israel and Judah had been a "curse" among the nations, God would now make them instead a "blessing." It is significant that God addressed both Judah and Israel and not just the returned Judeans. This would bear out the picture that Ezekiel traced in 37:15–22, where the divided kingdom of Israel and Judah would be reunited as one revived nation, under one God and one rule of the Messiah himself.

G. Do we believe God wants us to speak the truth, to render sound judgment and not to plot evil against our neighbor? (8:14–17)

Our Lord had been true to his word in carrying out his threats; therefore, he will be just as faithful in carrying out his promises. He would not prove false to his word on either account—in his judgments or in his promises. But if one is to benefit from any of these great promises of our Lord, he or she must respond in faith and obedience.

To help us realize how to do this, our Lord noted some of the key areas. He wanted his people to: speak the truth to one's neighbor, render true and sound judgment in our courts, not plot evil against each other, and not love false oaths. All who oppose this teaching enter into things that God detests and hates (v. 16). Thus, we and our leaders, our judges, and/or elders had better be careful, for God keeps careful records.

Are We Ready for the Future – 8:18–22

Finally, the answer to the question given in 7:3 is now given in explicit terms. The Lord himself listed the four new fast days that Israel had added to the liturgy of the Temple. They included:

The Fasts Days:	To Commemorate:
A fast in the fourth month	to recall the taking of the city of Jerusalem
A fast on the fifth month	to recall the destruction of the city and Temple
A fast on the seventh month	to recall the murder of Governor Gedaliah
A fast on the tenth month	to recall the commencement of the siege of Zion

Instead, the Lord promised these days would become days and occasions of joy and gladness. Therefore, he urged that the people to love truth and peace (v. 19), for the long night of weeping would be followed by the morning of joy and rejoicing.

The promise was that "many peoples and many cities" (20) would one day say, "let us go at once to entreat the LORD and seek the LORD Almighty" (v. 21), just as Isaiah 2:2–3 and Micah 4: 1–3 had predicted. All the nations of the world will flow into Jerusalem to be taught of the Lord. However, some allegorizing commentators improperly argue that the literal fulfillment of this passage is a sheer impossibility, as if this text had not warned that all of this would seem impossible / wonderful / marvelous (8:6). Yes, hordes of people and the powerful nations (v. 22) will come to Jerusalem to worship the Lord God. In fact, "ten people from all languages and nations will take firm hold of one Jew by the hem of his garment and say, 'Let us go with you, because we have heard that God is with you'" (v. 23). Thus, as Ruth expressed it, Israel's God will be our God, and her people will be our people, and we will go with you. In that day the Jewish people will be one with God, thus Gentiles will want to be one with Israel to be one with God.

Conclusions

1. Too often we have served ourselves rather than serving God.

2. Too often the routine of worship was there, but little or no real worship of the Living God was taking place.

3. Too often we have offered mere attendance at the house of God for a real meeting with him. Physical presence is no substitute for heartfelt obedience and awesome worship of the Living God!

4. Too often we have been reluctant to believe that the zeal of the Lord of Hosts will do what he said he would do to the enemies of Israel.

5. Too often we have failed to believe that God will restore Israel back to her land and that Jerusalem will once again be re-inhabited to the full and serve as a teaching center of God's word in that coming day!

6. Too often we have doubted that the nations will gather in Jerusalem to be taught of the Lord.

Lesson 10

Arriving with the Messianic King in Jerusalem Who Will Govern the Kingdom of God
Zechariah 9:1–10:1

Introduction to the Fourth Block of Text: Zechariah 9–14

The fourth and final block of messages in Zechariah covers the last six chapters of the book—9 to 14. These are divided into two equal chapters: 9–11 and 12–14. Each main block is introduced with the formula: "The burden of the word of the LORD" (9:1; 12:1). In general, the first "burden" emphasizes the first coming of our Lord, while the second "burden" has as its main theme the second coming of Messiah to this earth. Moreover, the first burden describes the rejection of the Messianic "Shepherd" (11:4–17), while the second one demonstrates how Messiah will finally be recognized by Israel as a massive renewal takes place among the people (12:10–13:10). The tone of this fourth block of texts changes from the earlier portions, yet the chapters are not unrelated to the content of the previous eight.

He Will Be Preceded by the Onslaught of Alexander the Great's Victories – 9:1–8

The first coming of our Lord will be set up in many ways by the overwhelming conquests of the Macedonian General named "Alexander the Great" in the fourth century BCE That is why the form this prophecy takes is accurately called a "burden," a noun from the Hebrew root *nasa`*, "to lift up." Therefore, this was a message that carried a threat and an admonition. It was not an "oracle," as too many English translations incorrectly say! Instead, it carried a heavy message of judgment.

This prophecy begins with a word against the land of "Hadrach," a name that only occurs here in Scripture. At one time, this term was a real mystery, but it can now be identified as the Hatarika, which is mentioned in the Annals of the Assyrian kings as an Aramean country near Damascus and Hamath, on the Orontes River, against which Assyria campaigned in 772, 755, and 733 BCE

Thus, the general region of Damascus is named as the area where the prophet envisions a coming battle in the hinterland of the Anti-Lebanon mountains near Damascus and Syria. In fact, that is what later happened at the battle of Issus in southeastern Asia Minor in October of 333 BCE Alexander the Great inflicted a heavy defeat on Darius and the Persians, which then opened all of Syria and Canaan to his blitzkrieg style of warfare. The prophet had indeed envisioned the defeat of Judah's traditional enemies: first Damascus, Hamath, and then the cities such as Tyre and Sidon inside the Syrian interior along the coast.

A detachment of Alexander's army conquered Hadrach, with its key towns, Damascus and Hamath, as the prophet pictured "the eyes of all the people" (v. 1), along with the eyes of "all the tribes of Israel," which were focused on the Lord. This meant that when the eyes of all the Gentiles and Israel gazed on what Alexander was doing, they were focusing on the Lord who was behind all that was going on through Alexander's armies.

Verses 2b–4 focused on Tyre and Sidon, singled out because of their great wealth, prosperity and worldly wisdom. Tyre's opulence and pride was so overbearing that Ezekiel gave an extended treatment of such contempt in 28:2–8, 11–19. The name Tyre comes from the Hebrew *tsor*, "rock," which she had built for herself as a "bulwark/stronghold" (Hebrew *matsor*, a pun).

Tyre had such wealth that its silver was said to be heaped up like dust and her gold was like "mire," or "mud," in the streets (v. 3).

The secular historian Diodorus Siculus noted that Nebuchadnezzar had been unsuccessful in his thirteen years of attempting to lay siege and conquer Tyre, as had the Assyrian King Shalmaneser, who likewise proved unsuccessful in his earlier five-year siege. But Tyre, in a haughty manner, simply picked up all her stuff and moved one half mile out in the Mediterranean Sea to an island fortification, where she made a new city for herself. Moreover, they surrounded insular Tyre with a wall 150 feet high, so she felt secure. But Alexander was not to be denied a victory over proud Tyre. He merely scraped up the ruins of the ruined mainland city, dumped its timbers, stones and rubbish into the Mediterranean, and built a causeway, or mole, out into the sea. He marched his army and siege machines over the mole and took the unconquerable Tyre in 332 BCE It took only seven months—an improvement on Shalmaneser's five years and Nebuchadnezzar's eleven years of failed sieges.

Few prophecies in the Old Testament are fulfilled more dramatically than this one about Tyre (cf. Ezek. 26:12). In fact, this passage in Ezekiel literally says:

> They will break down your walls and demolish your fine houses and
> throw your stones, timber and rubble into the sea.

Alexander was clearly given divine wisdom and an impressive strategy from God himself, for v. 4 introduced this concept with an interjectional adverb, "'Look/Behold' the Lord will take away her possessions and destroy her power on the sea, and she will be consumed by fire." Hence the Lord "drove out" the Tyrians and took possession of their commercial island-center. The mole that Alexander created was never removed but was covered with sand deposits so that it remains to this very day.

Alexander moved from conquering the northern sites of Phoenicia to take on the southern cities of Philistia. Four of the five Philistine Pentapolises are named here: Ashkelon, Ashdod, Ekron and Gaza; the city of Gath is usually omitted because it belonged, at least for a time, to Judah. No special details of Alexander's march against Ashdod, Ekron or Ashdod are given here, but the outcome of the battle for Gaza is fully and unmercifully recorded. Gaza's king, Batis, was ruthlessly slain as he was dragged through the streets, attached to a chariot with thongs thrust through the soles of his feet. Ten thousand of Gaza's inhabitants were slaughtered as well.

Batis was called a king, for the Persians had allowed Gaza's own local ruler to be a sort of sub-king under the Persian monarch, who was the "king of kings." However, God would cut off the "pride of the Philistines," and "a mongrel people will occupy Ashdod," God said (v. 6). He would also take away the "blood" of the idolatrous sacrifices of the Philistines (v. 7). Thus, as judgment fell on Israel's neighboring enemies, God would "encamp" around his people to protect them and reserve them for the coming of the Messiah.

There is a rather remarkable fulfillment of the first part of v. 8 recorded in Josephus' *Antiquities of the Jews* (XI.8:3). It happened that Alexander had demanded of the Jewish High Priest Jaddua the customary tribute Judah had paid to the Persian king. But Jaddua refused to break his oath of loyalty to the Persian King Darius, so Alexander threatened severe punishments on Jerusalem. He would carry out his threats after he finished dealing with Tyre and the Philistine cities.

But Jaddua ordered the people of Jerusalem to make sacrifices to God and to pray for deliverance from Alexander. God gave Jaddua a dream in which he was instructed to go out of the city of Jerusalem to welcome Alexander, so he did. Thus, the Macedonian conqueror was met by the Jewish High Priest clothed in purple and scarlet, with a miter on his head made with its golden plate and the name of God inscribed on it. He was followed by priests clothed in white robes.

Amazingly enough, Alexander also spoke of having had a dream prior to this event, in which he saw such a person when he was at Dios in Macedonia. Consequently, Alexander treated the Jews kindly, and Jerusalem was granted the self-same deliverance Zechariah had relayed in his prophecy in v. 8. God himself had announced that he would "encamp about his house because of an army." His "house" stood for the whole land of Israel or his people living in that land. The "army," of course, was that of Alexander the Great. Thus, Judah was supernaturally spared by two dreams given to two different leaders—one to Jaddua and the other to Alexander!

He Will Come at His First Arrival as a Humble King and Savior – 9:9 – 10:1

Verses 1–8 trace the victorious progress of the Gentile world conqueror, Alexander the Great, whom God would use as his rod of chastisement on Israel's enemies while delivering the people and land of Israel by encamping around about them. Thus, at the heart of chapter 9 stands one of the most famous predictions about the coming of the Messianic king. As such, it functions as the pivotal point between vv. 1–8 and 11–17.

The prophet begins by urging the people of Jerusalem, here personified as "the daughter of Zion" and "the daughter of Jerusalem," to "rejoice greatly" and "shout" (v. 9). The reason for all this commotion is that earth will finally receive the first coming of her king. Previously, the prophet Zechariah has issued the same call for jubilation in Zechariah 3:14–15: "Sing, O daughter of Zion! Shout, O Israel. … The King of Israel is in your midst." That same word was in Zechariah 2:10 as well. His arrival would be cause for heaps of joy!

But with the word about his appearing came a description of the character of this coming royal Messiah (v. 9d–f). First, he would be "righteous," i.e., one who would be animated by maintaining and displaying his righteous rule with justice and fairness all the time. Second, he would come "having salvation." Here, the verb is used in its passive form, meaning the Messiah has experienced the Father's deliverance and victory. Third, Messiah would be described as "lowly," one showing "humility" and identity with the poor and disenfranchised. To illustrate this, Messiah would come "riding on a donkey, on a colt, the foal of a donkey." Contrary to how the donkey is regarded in the West, in the ancient Near East the donkey was not thought of as a lowly beast of burden but as a preferred mount of princes (Judg. 5:10; 10:4; 12;14), or the mount of kings (2 Sam. 16:1–2). Horses, especially when hitched to chariots, were viewed as instruments of war

(Deut. 17:16; Ps. 33:16–17; Isa. 33:1). Therefore, the fact that Messiah did not come at his first arrival on a horse signified that he would not come, at least at this time, as a conqueror. Instead, he would come as promised in Genesis 49:11 mounted on a donkey. His coming would signal peace in the latter days to come and for all eternity.

Two of the synoptic gospels, Matthew 21:2–7 and John 12:12–15, connect this prophecy with the triumphal entry of Yeshua into Jerusalem on Palm Sunday. John notes that Yeshua rode on the "young" animal, while Matthew notes that both the donkey and the colt were brought for Yeshua's use. As he would later enter Jerusalem, the crowds would shout "Hosanna, save now!" They would cut down branches and spread their coats out as a carpet for Yeshua to ride on. This prophecy would be literally fulfilled—and that is what happened!

He Will Come in His Second Arrival to Establish His World-Wide Kingdom – 9:10–17

After treating the first arrival of Yeshua to Jerusalem, we turn to our Lord's second arrival in vv. 10–17. Immediately, our Lord calls for the abolishment of three weapons of war: "the chariots from Ephraim," "the war-horses from Jerusalem," and "the battle bow" (v. 10). God's kingdom would not be founded on worldly might or military power, for the Prince of Peace certainly would not be delivered from those who were hostile to him by means of chariots and horses and their armies. The mention of "Ephraim" and "Jerusalem" was but one more reminder that the northern and southern kingdoms of the Israelite kingdom, split apart since 931 BCE, would be reunified and restored once again.

The Prince of Peace would not only benefit Israel and Judah, but "he shall proclaim peace to the nations" (v. 10d) as well. The result would be that "his rule will extend from sea to sea and from the River (i.e., the Euphrates) to the ends of the earth" (v. 10e–f). This is quoting Psalm 72. His kingdom would extend over the whole globe! It would be worldwide!

The last seven verses of the ninth chapter discuss the results and mission of the Redeemer-King, especially as they pertain to Israel nationally. The section begins with "As for you" (v. 11a), which links 11–13 with 9–10. And everything that will happen in that future day—the arrival of Messiah and his rule and reign as absolute Lord over all—will have been made possible by "the blood of my covenant" (v. 11a), a phrase that occurs only one other time in Scripture, Exodus 24:8, though the Old Testament referred often to the idea of a blood sacrifice when the covenant was ratified with Abraham (e.g., Gen. 15:9–11) or with Moses (Ex. 24:8). These words, however, are familiar to us; Yeshua used them at the Last Supper: "This is my blood of the new covenant, which is shed for many" (Mk. 14:24). What then did the "blood" refer to?

Blood in these contexts does not refer as it does in our modern times to a transfusion that would impart sustained life; instead, it signifies that the life was in the blood (Lev. 17:11) and that which was spilt on the ground in death as a substitute for those whose debt was paid for by the one presenting the sacrificial offering.

Because of the substituted life that has been yielded up on our behalf, God promises to "will free your prisoners from the waterless pit" (v. 11b). This reference to the "waterless pit" was odd to some, but the point was, as there were no jails in that day, cisterns normally used to collect rainwater during the rainy season also often had to double at times as a retention center, or a jail for the convicted felons. Thus, Joseph was cast into a "pit" that had no water in it (Gen. 37:24), as was the prophet Jeremiah (Jer. 38:6–13). But our Lord promises to empty these pits or jails. Those so released, Zechariah dubs "prisoners of hope" (v. 12a). They will surely return to the "fortress," i.e., to Zion once again. In so doing, God will "restore twice as much to [them]" (v. 12b), just as the "firstborn" would receive a double inheritance (Deut. 21:17).

God would involve Judah and Ephraim in his liberation of the captives. He would rouse Zion's sons against the sons of Greece/Javan (v. 13c), a prediction of the Maccabean wars in a later period of Israel's history. But the Lord will protect his people under the figure of a storm (v. 14).

The chapter closes with a description of a banquet for the released prisoners. The odd language has led some to incorrectly think the prisoners were consuming the flesh and/or blood of their enemies. But the eating and drinking in this context are metaphors for celebrating God's victory over the nations. Likewise, the "sling stones" (v. 15) are mere reminders of previous battles, which are now no more than gravel to be trampled underfoot.

The food will be so abundant at the victory celebration that "they will drink and roar as with wine" (v. 15c). In fact, the tables will be so full of food that they will look like an altar appears when the meat on it overflows even into the corners of the altar.

Verse 16a continued by saying, "On that day," ADONAI will save his people, and as a result his "flock" will be safe. They will "sparkle in his land like jewels in a crown." Here was another metaphor from Exodus 19:5, where the believing remnant would be God's "treasured possession," which signified moveable treasures as opposed to real estate that could not be moved (cf. Mal. 3:17). Together, grain and wine would be abundant in that day. Evil will have been vanquished forever and the Lord God would be in charge (Amos 9:13; Joel 3:18).

Yes, the prosperity of those days would depend on rain, so 10:1 urged the people of God to "ask the LORD for rain in the time of the latter rain" (10:1). The promise was if the people asked, the Lord would send showers of rain and there would be plants from the field for everyone. This would be a different day indeed!

Conclusions

1. What a difference everything will be when the Messiah king comes exhibiting righteousness. He will exemplify a paid-for salvation and a humility of purpose as he rides into Jerusalem on a donkey.

2. What an even greater difference will it make when the Messiah comes a second time as king of kings and Lord of lords.

3. Alexander the Great may have opened up the way for Messiah, but his victories would pale in comparison to the victories of King Yeshua over all nations.

4. Messiah would come as the Prince of Peace for all Israel and for all the nations.

Lesson 11

Contrasting the Guidance Given by the False and True Shepherds of Israel
Zechariah 10:2–12

Zechariah introduces a new metaphor in chapters 10–11—the metaphor of the "shepherd" as leader. The word "shepherd" in its ancient Near Eastern setting was not a novel concept, for it was often used to designate any number of leadership positions; it was used to illustrate the position of teacher, priest, judge, ruler, king, governor, or the like.

However, it was all too easy to turn such a privileged position into an opportunity to abuse others. The people, in this case, were likened to "sheep," which were powerless to do anything to help themselves in such situations. Moreover, leaders all too frequently looked in the wrong direction for their guidance and assistance to the people. For example, it was all too common for a leader to look to their own idols for the alleged wisdom they needed to direct and lead the people. This could mean only trouble ahead for the people and leaders alike.

Let's look at Zechariah 10 and see how the shepherd was depicted.

The Contrasts Between the Corrupted Shepherds and the Compassionate Shepherds – 10:2–5

The land of Canaan was known as "the land of milk and honey," yet for such a blessing to be observed, Israel was nevertheless exhorted to "ask" for it, even though God had promised that the land would become like the garden of Eden (Ezek. 36:37). This text meant literal rain, yet it did not avoid involving in that same request the great spiritual blessings that could come as part of a similar request. Both the physical and spiritual blessings were dependent on the hand of God (Jer. 14:22).

Over the centuries, it became increasingly clear that it was God who could withhold the rainfall, regardless of the secondary causes. He would call on men and women to ask him for rain so that the scorching summer sun would not devastate the land during the dry seasons of the year.

Thus, there was in chapters 9 and 10 a blending of both temporal and spiritual blessings, as the rain and blessing came from asking God.

But when Israel turned away from the Lord and depended on idols, or *teraphim*, they trusted in deceitful counselors and pagan diviners instead of listening to the word from God. In total there are eight passages in the Hebrew Bible where the *teraphim* are discussed (e.g., Gen. 31:19; Judg. 17:5, 18:5; 1 Sam. 15:23). These were not just idols; they were also used for obtaining oracular responses from the evil one. For example, the *teraphim* appear in connection with Jacob's flight from Laban in Genesis 30. Some interpreters argue that Rachel stole them from Laban to discover directions from these oracles for their flight (a sort of ancient version of a GPS), but archaeologists insist that possession of the *teraphim* was an indication that their owner was the inheritor of property. Elsewhere, we get another glimpse of the heart condition of some of the tribes of Israel when the Ephraimite Micah lost his *teraphim*; the tribe of Dan stole them from Micah as they were moving to Laish/Dan in northern Israel.

As if that were not bad enough, these leaders taught their people to put their trust in diviners, even though these evil sources offered them nothing but lies, as they told false dreams (v. 2b–c). The problem was not with the fact that these diviners used dreams, for God frequently used dreams to communicate with his people; the issue was that their dreams were false and spun out of their own imagination so that they gave comfort "in vain" (v. 2d). Some of these charlatans would also shoot down birds to inspect their entrails to determine what "auspices," or course of action, they should take (Josh. 13:22; 1 Sam. 6:2). It was an outright denial of God's revealed will.

As a result of this misdirected leadership, "the people wander[ed] like sheep" (v. 2e). Since there were only unreliable and false sources of leadership, the people were in effect without a shepherd (v. 2f). They had no true shepherd who cared for them and who would lead them!

Such defiance made God's anger burn against these false shepherds (v. 3a), who could count on being punished by him (v. 3b). Israel, having lost her native rulers, fell instead under the power of heathen governors, here styled as "shepherds" or "he-goats" (Hebrew `atudim*). In Ezekiel 34:17, the "he-goats" are sharply distinguished from the Lord's "sheep." The bellwether was the sheep that led the flock with a bell on its neck, another apt figure for a leader. Thus, God himself will punish the false shepherds and he-goats as he "visits" his flock to make them instead "like a proud horse/steed in battle" (v. 3e).

God would cure Israel's deception as Messiah will come as the "cornerstone," "tent-pin" and "war-bow" (v. 4). Let's examine each title.

Messiah as the Cornerstone. The prophet has in mind Isaiah 28:16, "See I lay a stone in Zion, a tested stone, a precious *cornerstone* for a sure foundation; the one who relies on it will never be stricken with panic." The Hebrew *pinnah*, "cornerstone," is without the article as *tsemach*, "Branch," was in 3:8, 6:12. Messiah came as the "cornerstone" to his people Israel, but they regarded him as "a stumbling stone" (Rom. 9:32, 33; 1 Cor. 1:23) and as a "rock of Offense" over which they tripped and stumbled! But the people of God in the church found that Messiah was indeed "the foundation," "the chief cornerstone" (Eph. 2:19–22). Indeed, Messiah is the angle at which Jew and Gentile meet and are united into one building. Thus, Messiah is not only the foundation on which the truth of God is built, but he is also the cornerstone in which the two walls unite at the corner and are joined together.

Messiah as the Tent-Pin. The Hebrew *yated*, "tent-stake" or "tent-pin," is used first as the stake driven into the ground to hold up the ropes of the tent. But this same term is also used for the strong peg inside the Oriental tent, upon which is hung the most important implements. The primary allusion made here is to Isaiah 22:22–25…

> I will place on his shoulder the key to the house of David; what he opens no one can shut, and what he shuts, no one can open. I will drive him like a peg into a firm place; he will become the seat of honor for the house of his father. All the glory of his family will hang on him: its offspring and offshoots—all its lesser vessels, from the bowls to all the jars. In that day, declares the LORD Almighty, the peg driven into the firm place will give way; it will be sheared off and will fall, and the load hanging on it will be cut down. The LORD has spoken.

This prophecy in Isaiah was given about one of the sons of David known as Eliakim, but it also merges into a prophecy about the Messiah. It is Messiah who will sit on the glorious throne of his Father's house, for he alone will be the One who will be the true heir and perpetuator of the throne of his Father. They will hang on it all that pertains to Messiah, just as they hang on the "Tent-Pin" every vessel that has essential use for the running of a household—small and great, all the glory of the Father's house is at the ready on the tent-pin. Only in Messiah will all the glory of the Father's house be suspended and there for all to see! When a person walked into an Oriental tent, the wealth of the occupant of that household was hung on that tent-peg both for ornamentation and for admiration, but also for its utilization. So, it will come to pass when Messiah shall bear the glory and sit and rule on his throne (Zech. 6:13) in all his millennial splendor.

Eliakim was God's faithful servant who succeeded the faithless Shebna. Therefore, he would be like a peg that was fastened in a secure place. But even he, faithful though he was, died by virtue of old age, sickness and death. But the true Seed of David, the God-man, would be the only dependable tent Peg who will not fail. His rule will be permanent and his authority imperishable (Isa. 9:7).

Messiah the Battle-Bow. The Hebrew term for this new metaphor for Messiah is *qeshet milchamah*, "battle-bow." In this figure, Messiah is spoken of as a Warrior and Conqueror; he would be the divine archer who at his second coming would drive his arrows into the hearts of his enemies. In Revelation, Messiah is depicted as riding astride a white horse making war on the nations (19:11). Verse 4, with three pictures of Messiah as the model leader, ends with "from him every ruler [together]" would go forth, for Messiah would be the source of all such compassionate leaders. By the work of Messiah, every oppressor will depart from Israel, no matter the means.

The Contrast Between the Nation's Former State and the Future Regathering of the Jewish People in Their Land – 10:5–12

The Lord promises to be with his people (v. 5) in that future day as he empowers his people to overthrow all false leaders and oppressors. So expertly will Israel push back against her attackers that even the most exalted cavalry will be handily defeated and embarrassed.

The events anticipated here are those of the battle of Armageddon (Rev. 16:14; 19:17–20). The "beast" (Dan. 7:8) seems to push his invasion against Israel from the north, but the Lord has promised to be with his people. Instead, the Lord will strengthen his people (6, 12), even though this battle must conclude with the glorious appearance of Messiah on earth.

God promises to "bring back/restore" (v. 6c) his people into the land. This amazing prediction was made some time after December 7, 518 BCE (Zech. 7:1). If these prophecies are in chronological order, this is almost 20 years after the return from the Babylonian exile had commenced. Moreover, this was not just a promise made about the Judean captives in Babylon; it also involved those who had been taken into the Assyrian captivity in 721 as the reference to the "tribes of Joseph" demonstrates (vv. 6b, 7, 10). God would "hear them" (v. 6f) and he would "answer them."

God promises he will "signal/whistle" (Hebrew *sharaq*) for his people as he gathered them in (v. 8a; cf. Isa. 5:26, 27; 7:18, 19). The shrill call noted here was not simply the calling together of insects as a beekeeper might use;

it is used typically of shepherds who "piped" on their rough reed pipes a gathering signal for his scattered flock to reassemble around their shepherd. Instinctively, the sheep, goats or cows would assemble and prepare to follow their shepherd, for they recognized the piped tune or whistle.

In this figurative way, our Lord would likewise "redeem" his people from sin, but he would also bring them out of the diaspora, whereby they had been scattered all over the world. As a result, they would increase their number (v. 8d) and become as numerous as they had been previously. Just as it happened in the Egyptian bondage (Exod. 1:7), so it has happened time after time in Europe, Russia, and other parts of the world— the more they were afflicted, the more they multiplied.

In verse 10c–d, God declared he would bring his people Israel into the "land of Gilead and Lebanon and there will be no room enough for them." It is said that the French atheist Voltaire scoffed as he also blasphemed God by saying that since God gave the Jews a land no larger than Wales, he must therefore be a small God. In verse 10, Gilead and Lebanon are also included in the land deeded over to the Jewish nation for the future. "Gilead" has primary reference to what is called today the "Golan Heights," and "Lebanon" encompassed such coastal cities as Tyre, Sidon, Beirut and Byblos. Thus, the Holy land reaches out in a northeasterly direction to the Euphrates up through the Damascus corridor. Even with all of this, there will not be enough room for all the Jewish people who will be brought back into the land. There are many millions of Jews back in the land of Israel already, or nearly half of the worldwide population of Jews. This was one of the key signs that the return of the Lord was near!

The Lord will remove every impediment that would potentially block the way of Israel's full restoration and return to the land (v. 11). Zechariah needed only refer to the marvelous interventions of the Lord in days past to predict an even greater deliverance in the days to come. The "sea of affliction / trouble" (v. 11a) and all the "depths of the Nile will dry up" (v. 11c). But these obstacles will prove no problem for such a great God. This prophecy ends in chapter 10 almost with a signature appended to the whole work: The name of the Lord is the sign, seal and certainty that all will be fulfilled.

Conclusions

1. The contrasts in this passage are striking to say the least. A false and unreliable leader/shepherd has nothing to compare with a compassionate and wise shepherd.

2. How could anyone ever think that the false and ruthless shepherds/ "he-goats" were any match for the Living God?

3. The Good Shepherd will be known as Israel's "Cornerstone," "Tent-Peg" and "Battle-Bow," for he will be a victorious Deliverer.

4. God promised to "whistle" one more time for all the Jewish people to re-gather as he would restore them to their land and enlarge it into Lebanon and Gilead.

Lesson 12

Expecting the Destruction of Israel Because of Her Rejection of the Good Shepherd

Zechariah 11:1–17

Zechariah 11 is generally considered one of the most difficult, enigmatic passages in the Old Testament to interpret. The passage is difficult because it speaks of a "flock" that is doomed to be slaughtered, but is the "flock" the nation of Israel, or the nations of the world? And who is the "shepherd"? Is he the prophet Zechariah taking the role of the shepherd of Israel, or does he represent a divinely appointed leader who has been (or will be) rejected by the people of the land? Then, who is the good shepherd who is rejected in verses 15–17 in favor of a "foolish shepherd"? These are some of the questions that make this passage difficult.

Assuredly, Zechariah, whose name means "whom the Lord remembers," is a prophet of hope as seen in the messages he has given thus far in this book. His vision spans the centuries, yet it centers on Israel and her future as it is to be realized in her coming Savior, King, and Deliverer. Zechariah 9 and 10 dwell on the joyous theme of Messiah's coming, and it also shows how the nations surrounding Israel would then be judged, while Israel will be preserved and her land will be restored.

But suddenly, this prophet of hope and good news becomes a reality check as he gives us glimpses of the tragedy that will beset the nation of Israel because of her apostasy, as seen most graphically in her rejection of the good Shepherd (11:1–14) and her acceptance of a worthless shepherd instead (vv. 15–17). Israel rejected their true Messianic Shepherd at the time of his first arrival. But even more horrifying is the fact that in the time of their greatest woe and sorrow, they will take up with a false shepherd just before the second coming of their Messiah and Deliverer.

True, in the first part of Zechariah's prophecy (chapters 1–8), "the good and comfortable words" (1:13) form the essence and the theme of most of the eight night-visions (1:7– 6:8). But this prophet of hope is also one of truth and reality, so he now records words that are starkly tragic and filled with ominous gloom. They will form the prelude to the glorious blessings that must follow, but this dark and ominous storm must precede the bursting forth of the day of God's deliverance and resplendent appearance in glory! So how does all of this come about?

The Collapse of the National Shepherds – 11:1–3

Right from the get-go in this chapter we are introduced to tragedy and a dark note as a warning of the awful events that must be narrated here. The words are used in such graphic poetic forms that they stir up vivid images and dramatic movements. One can almost feel the impact of the awfulness of the events depicted here, for judgment must be visited upon the land because Israel's outright rejection of the good shepherd is so uncalled-for.

Verses 1–3 are a short poem that focus on the collapse of Lebanon (to the north of Israel) as well as the land of Bashan (known also as the Golan Heights) in the area northeast of the Sea of Galilee and leading to the corridor through Damascus up to the Euphrates River.

Lebanon was renowned for its majestic cedar trees, while Bashan was equally renowned for its oaks. However, despite such prominence, both the cedars and the oaks would experience the humiliation of being leveled, just as all national pride must likewise give way to the sweeping hand of God's judgment on these nations and their leaders.

Thus, the prophet sighs over how such mighty cedars and oaks could have fallen. What was going to happen to the trees becomes a metaphor for the complete devastation of the countryside.

Mount Lebanon, with its 14,000-foot height on the border of Syria and Canaan, perpetually had its peak covered with snow. It was known as "the white one," or as the Arabs preferred to call it, "the mountain of snow." The mountain was to throw open its doors, giving access to the decimating fire that would ravage the land and its majestic cedars. Imagine what could be expected for the "juniper/cypress" trees. Thus, the humbler tree joins in the lament for the advancing destruction.

Bashan was bounded in the south by the wadi Jabbak and Mount Gilead (Deut. 3:10; Josh. 12:4), a territory taken from the Amorite King of Og by the invading Israelites and given to the half tribe of Manasseh (Num 21:33; 32:33). As the fiery conflagration sweeps down over the pasture lands, it is time for the shepherds to wail as well (v. 3a–b). The fire rages even down the Jordan valley, for in the jungle-growth there, south of the Sea of Galilee, a roar is heard from the lions as they see their favorite haunts in the luxurious grasses, willows, tamarisks and cane consumed by fire (v. 3c–d).

Since no known event in the regular course of history seems to fit what is described here, these events must describe something yet to come. Verses 1–3 may well describe the collapse of all the nations surrounding Israel in that final day connected with the second return of the Lord. Therefore, we await the appearance of the actual events to untangle the mystery found in these verses.

The Rejection of the Good Shepherd – 11:4–14

Once again, this is a difficult section to interpret. A shepherd is instructed to look after a flock of sheep that has been slated for slaughter. It seems the prophet is to act out a parable or a drama that has prophetic truth to it. He therefore dresses in the garb of a shepherd and assumes both a religious and a civic function as he discharges this commission.

The text switches to a prose narrative in verses 4–14 as the Lord gives the instructions (v. 4a). "Feed the flock for slaughter," the Lord directs. And the prophet writes: "So I shepherded the flock marked for slaughter." Though this may be a symbolic action like the actions of other prophets (e.g., Mic. 1:8), there are "three shepherds" in addition to the prophet (11:8). And the extended nature of the comparison noted here seems to point to something more than a parable or an allegory taking place here. The ruthless leaders did not seem to care whether the people lived or died; they were merely sheep destined for the slaughter.

Verse 5 continued the imagery of these miserable, worthless shepherds who saw the flock merely as a commodity by which they could make money. Thus, God's people, his flock, as well as others were suffering under the hands of these sheep merchants, who were only interested own self-enrichment. So they slaughtered the flock without any feelings of guilt. These sheep merchants would piously say, "Praise the LORD/Blessed be the LORD, for I am rich" (v. 5b). They had no more concern for the flock than did the hireling in John 10:13. The sheep merchants here were likely the foreign rulers who felt no guilt over what they did or allowed, for they trafficked humans as slaves, a practice the prophet strongly decried (Amos 1:6). Meanwhile, "their own shepherds do not spare them" (v. 5d), for the Jewish leaders likewise abandoned God's flock, an act just as reprehensible as the profiteering of the foreign shepherds.

In verse 6, the Lord speaks out once again; what could God's people expect to happen? It was a decisive word: "I will no longer have pity on the people of the land" (v. 6a). What an announcement! Instead, God would "give everyone into the hands of his neighbors" (v. 6b). He would hand the whole land of Israel over into the hands of foreign kings and wicked shepherds. But then the wicked shepherds and the sinful citizens of the land would find themselves in a position where they were powerless to defend themselves. These foreign kings would attack the land, but the most tragic note is this: God would "not rescue anyone from their hands" (v. 6d).

What was Zechariah to do considering this judgment? He would become Israel's shepherd despite the certain doom that loomed. He would be the shepherd "particularly [of] the oppressed of the flock" (v. 7). The interpretation of this clause has been hotly debated, for even though this is the correct reading of the Hebrew text and of the Jewish Targums, the Greek Septuagint rendering of this phrase takes a more difficult reading: "for the Canaanites/merchants," i.e., the "sheep merchants."

Zechariah shepherded his flock with two staffs, one named "Beauty/Grace/Favor" and the other "Bonds/Union." These tools of a shepherd, his rod and his staff, are here transformed into two staffs, which give us an insight into the shepherd's ministry: His desire for the flock was that they might enjoy God's favor and experience national unity. But this hope was not to be realized by Israel in Zechariah's time.

To call verse 8 difficult is an understatement. There are some 40 conjectures as to who the three shepherds are. The text merely says that in one month, he had to dismiss three shepherds (v. 8). Some point to the three Judean kings that formed the Davidic dynasty: Jehoiakim, Jehoiachin and Zedekiah—all in a short amount of time! But it does no good to speculate.

Zechariah's patience with the flock of Israel was beginning to run out as "the flock detested [him]" and he "grew weary of them" (v. 8b). The prophet seemed ready to give up: "Let the dying die and the perishing perish" (v. 9b). Those remaining could just as well cannibalize each other (v. 9c), for that is what they would need to do as the severity of the famine was realized. And that happened not only in the siege of Jerusalem in 586 BCE, but in 70 CE as well. Couldn't the people see that Zechariah was acting on behalf of the people? Instead of recognizing the favor he had done for them by dismissing three shepherds, they turned on Zechariah, the good shepherd. That is when the prophet broke his staff "Favor" (v. 10a).

That action still brings up another hard text, indeed, one of the more difficult passages. Verse 10 speaks of the prophet "revoking the covenant … made with all the nations." How should the breaking of this covenant be interpreted, especially as God had promised as far back as Genesis 12:1–3, 15:1–6 that he would not break his covenant, but it would be an unconditional promise made with Abraham and David (2 Sam. 7:12–19)? The conditional covenant of Moses (Ex. 19–24) had already been broken by Israel, but which covenant was Zechariah talking about? The answer seems to be that the covenant mentioned is the one God made with the Gentile nations. Note the plural form of "nations" at the end of verse 10.

Verse 11 gives us the reaction of "the oppressed/poor of the flock that were watching that day" (v. 11b). These observers realized the breaking of this covenant was the result of God's judgment on the people for rejecting his appointed shepherd.

Zechariah, who is acting as the shepherd in this scene of symbolic actions, now requests his wages for the service he has rendered. Though he asks tentatively, perhaps because he has terminated his contract (v. 9), the question is whether he addressed the whole flock or just the sheep merchants. If the latter, then the prophet is paid by these traders some "thirty pieces of silver," the same price paid for a gored slave (Ex. 21:32). This was also the price Judas received for betraying Yeshua (Mt. 26:15, 27:9). That Matthew attributes this prophecy to Jeremiah rather than to Zechariah may be because Matthew saw Zechariah combining Zechariah 11:12–13 with Jeremiah 18:1–4; 32:6–9. Thus, Matthew cited the more prominent prophet, which in this case would have been Jeremiah.

Verse 13 has a note of sarcasm, for Zechariah is told to "throw ... this handsome / princely price at which they valued me ... to the potter." Since the Hebrew words for "potter" (yotser) and "treasury" (`osar) sound alike, and as both ideas are found in Matthew 27:6–9, many have adopted the Syrian emendation of this text and read: "Throw it to the treasury." But that is not necessary, since the expression to "throw it to the potter" was a proverbial expression of contempt—"throw it away."

The money, however, was indeed cast into the house of the Lord (13d). The potter was connected to the Temple, for they made the sacrificial vessels (Lev. 6:28), so there may well have been a guild of potters who served on a regular basis at the house of God.

After he cast the thirty pieces of silver away, Zechariah broke the other staff, "Unity" (v. 14). The people had rejected their shepherd, so the national unity they had hoped for would not come about in their day. However, the prophet Ezekiel prophesied that there would come a day when they would be reunited under one shepherd who would take two sticks, one with the name of Joseph and one with the name of Judah, and "join them together into one stick" (Ezek. 37:16–28).

The Appointment of a Worthless Shepherd – 11:15–17

It is surprising to hear the Lord ask Zechariah to continue his role by impersonating a "worthless shepherd" (v. 15). His equipment would seem to be the same as those things used by a good shepherd, but the difference would be in the respective attitudes of the two shepherds toward the flock.

The explanation for this action appears in verse 16. God would raise up a shepherd who would not only neglect the duties that were expected of him as a shepherd, but his actions would also lead to the destruction of the flock. The savagery with which he would shepherd them was described as one who would "devour the flesh" of the sheep and "tear off their hooves" as he consumed them!

This chapter concludes with a poem (v. 17) that pronounces woe on such a worthless shepherd. His abandonment of the flock would not go unnoticed or unpunished by the Lord. The worthless shepherd is not identified in this chapter, but many Jewish commentators think it is King Herod (63–4 BCE), who was infamous for his brutal treatment of the Jewish people. Some think it is Alcimus (a High Priest in 163–59 BCE) who betrayed the Maccabees (1 Macc. 7:1–125). Others think that it is none other than the sinister figure of the Antichrist who will come in the final day (2 Thess. 2:1–12; Rev. 13:1–10).

Conclusions

1. What a shame that when the good Shepherd called to his flock, and wanted to continue his favor and unity, they turned away from him in disbelief and distrust. What a loss for them!

2. The hoped-for favor and unity for Israel will not come until the nation returns to the Lord in massive numbers at the second coming of Messiah.

3. The prophecy that the Good Shepherd would be sold for a trifling thirty pieces of silver, the price of a slave, underscores how expensive our salvation really is.

4. Judas is more than just a fall-character; he is the forerunner of all worthless shepherds to come and especially the Antichrist—that final one who will challenge Messiah.

Lesson 13

Experiencing God's Deliverance and a National Conversion in Israel
Zechariah 12:1–13:1

In the first of the two "burden" messages (Zech. 9–11) that make up the last six chapters of Zechariah, the prophet predicted that the Gentile powers and their nations would be destroyed as the kingdom of God came into its full manifestation as the stone that smashed all previous kingdoms (chapters 9–11). But with the overthrow of these Gentile world powers, Messiah's kingdom would be finally and fully established everywhere.

In the second "burden" message (12–14), Zechariah describes how Israel would be sifted and purged prior to the final conflict of earth's history as she faced the nations of the world alone. It is impossible to identify the calamities described in these chapters with the events, times and deeds that surrounded Nebuchadnezzar of Babylon—nor with those that fell on Israel as a result of Greco-Macedonian ruler Antiochus Epiphanes. None of the calamities mentioned end with Messiah appearing on the Mount of Olives in his second coming, as in the second set of burden messages. So the events in this second "burden" message can only be connected to the second appearing of our Lord that will come in that future day.

One of the key phrases in chapters 12–14 is "in that day," which occurs 17 times. This is another indication that the events described here belong to the time of the second coming of our Lord. Two other frequently occurring terms in these chapters are "Jerusalem," which appears 22 times, and "nations," which occurs 13 times.

God's Work in Conquering the Enemies of Israel – 12:1–9

The tragic and graphically told narrative (11:1–14) of Israel's rejection of the good shepherd in favor of a worthless one (Zech. 11:15–17) is now followed in chapter 12 by the description of the nation's divine deliverance and her future national conversion to the Lord. The fearful regime of the false shepherd provides one of the prompting reasons for Israel's future national conversion told in 12:1–13:8.

The Word of the Lord

The first "burden" message in Zechariah has already appeared in chapters 9–11 and focused on the first arrival of Messiah as the Shepherd-King. Now the second "burden" message (12–14) will focus on the second coming of Messiah as king over everything and the spectacular conversion of Israel to ADONAI her Lord.

All doubt is removed about the certitude of what is about to be announced, for it emanates distinctly from the mouth of the Lord himself. Moreover, we are reminded that this ADONAI is the very Lord God who showed his power in his creating everything in this universe, in his founding of the earth itself, and in his forming the very "spirit" of man (12:1). Zechariah's literary style here is remarkably similar at times to that of the prophet Isaiah. For example, he used three participial verbs to describe the omnipotence and the display of the power of God: the very same power of God that "stretched out" the heavens (Hebrew *noteh*), "laid" the foundation of the earth (*yosed*), and "formed" the human spirit within a person (*yotser*). These three verbs are reminiscent of texts such as Isaiah 42:5. This text refutes the deistic idea that originally God made the world in its basic materials and then left it to evolve for itself. But this text refuses to bow to such a fabricated theory, stating that God continued to work as both the heavens and the foundations of the earth were laid out by him alone, just as the human spirit of men and women was also a work of his hands!

The Day of the Lord

Suddenly God introduces a revolutionary word, for he begins with "Behold! Lo! Look here!" God is going to make Jerusalem a "cup of reeling/drunkenness" that will send all the surrounding nations reeling (12:2). This reference to a "cup of reeling" is usually a symbol of coming judgment and one that brings a condition of mortal helplessness like that of a person being intoxicated and helplessly staggering about. For example, even though the word for "cup" was not the same (Hebrew *saph*, "bowl," not *kos*, "cup,"), the concept is the same, as Psalm 75:8 warned:

> "In the hand of the LORD is a cup full of foaming wine mixed with spices; he pours it out, and all the wicked of the earth drink it down to its last dregs."

A similar theme is found in Isaiah 51:17, 22...

> "Awake, awake! Rise up O Jerusalem, you who have drunk from the hand of the LORD the cup of his wrath. ...This is what your sovereign LORD says, your God, who defends his people: See, I have taken out of your hand the cup that made you stagger; from that cup, the goblet of my wrath, you will never drink again."

Zechariah had used the Hebrew word for a "bowl," not a "cup," for a larger vessel was needed to allow all the nations to get drunk on its contents. But another point: God has now turned the tables. Israel will no longer suffer at the hand of her enemies. After Judah and Jerusalem have engaged in the battle of the ages, they are paired off against the nations of the entire world; that battle will be the end of her tasting this "cup of drunkenness/reeling" forever thereafter. Instead, in that final day, God will make Jerusalem "a cup that sends all the surrounding peoples reeling" as Judah is besieged along with the rest of Israel in that ultimate battle on earth. The phrase "On that day" appears in verses 3, 4, 6, 8, 9, and 11.

The Immovability of Jerusalem

There is coming a time ("On that day," 12:3) when "all the nations of the earth" will be "gathered against [Israel]." The magnitude of this final battle cannot be overemphasized. As John said in Revelation 16:14:

> "They are the demonic spirits that perform signs, and they go out to the kings of the whole world, to gather them for the battle on the great day of God Almighty."

Likewise, the prophet Joel saw a terribly similar happening yet to come:

> "In those days and at that time, when I restore the fortunes of Judah and Jerusalem, I will gather all nations and bring them down to the Valley of Jehoshaphat. There I will put them on trial for what they did to my inheritance, my people Israel, because they scattered my people among the nations and divided up my land." (Joel 3:1–2)

Some commentators believe Psalm 118:5–6, 10–12 apply directly or as types to the same situation in Judah and Jerusalem, as is described in Zechariah:

> "When hard pressed [same Hebrew word as "siege"],
> I cried to the LORD; he brought me into a spacious place.
> The LORD is with me;
> I will not be afraid.
> What can mere mortals do to me?
> All the nations surrounded me,
> but in the name of the LORD I will cut them down.
> They surrounded me on every side,
> but in the name of the LORD I will cut them down.
> They swarmed about me like bees,
> but they were consumed as quickly as burning thorns;
> in the name of the LORD I cut them down."

The city of Jerusalem will be "immovable rock"; it will prove to be such a "heavy stone" so that all who attempt to move it will "injure themselves," or to put it literally, they will "herniate themselves."

The Manner of God's Intervention to Rescue Judah and Jerusalem – 12:4–9

This decisive battle will take place "On that day" (v. 4a). This will be in the time when God's judgment will be poured out on the nations and when he will deliver Israel. Three Hebrew nouns describe how God will intervene to cause these three related situations: (1) "panic / confusion / bewilderment" (*timmahon*, from the root *tamah*, "to be dumbfounded," i.e., a "stupefaction"), (2) "madness" (*shigga'on*), and (3) "blindness" (*'iwwaron*). These three afflictions had been promised as judgments that would befall Israel, back as far as the times of Moses in Deuteronomy 28:28: "The LORD will afflict you with madness, blindness, and confusion of mind," if you walk contrary to his will and teaching.

God would "open his eyes on the house of Judah" (v. 4), perhaps the same look of love and pity that the Lord gave Peter in the Hall of Caiaphas when he denied him (Lk. 22:61–62), for this is what will melt the hearts of Israel in repentance and cause them to weep bitterly. This came at just the moment when Israel's enemies had thought that they had gained the upper hand and victory over Judah and Jerusalem was imminent in the final earthly battle. But at that same moment, God sent sudden confusion, bewilderment and panic among the nations.

With a sudden realization that ADONAI was indeed their God, Judah would turn on her enemy like a fire suddenly igniting dry tinder or ripen sheaves: Judah will be in that moment like a "firepot/firepan" in a woodpile" (v. 6). "They will consume all the surrounding peoples right and left, but Jerusalem will remain intact in her place" (v. 6c).

The inhabitants of Judah, who dwell in the countryside, will be delivered first, so the inhabitants of the house of David may not exalt themselves above Judah. All rivalry and division that might come both from either within or outside of the tribe will be discouraged. The invasion of the land of Israel is also described in this book, but it will come later in more detail in 13:8–9 and 14:1–6. For example, two-thirds of the people in the land will die, and one-half of Jerusalem will be carried away into captivity before the Lord steps into the battle. But his intervention will be mightily decisive. The fortunes of the battle will suddenly reverse in Israel's favor and to the confusion of her enemy.

God will shield/defend those living in Jerusalem (v. 8). This eschatological day will be one in which almost supernatural strength is suddenly given to the feeblest of those in Jerusalem (v. 8) so that they will act as valiantly and courageously as David did in the past. The once-broken and feeble Jewish remnant will recognize their divine Savior, and they shall shout for their king as never before!

This will be the time in the future when God will destroy all the nations that come to attack Jerusalem (v. 9). The expression used here in Hebrew is "I [God] will seek to destroy" (*'avaqqesh*, "to aim at") the enemy. But God also has a work he will do for Israel.

God's Work in Conquering the Hearts of Israel – 12:10–14

A marvelous happening takes place at this time, for the nation suddenly enjoys a great spiritual outpouring of God's Spirit as a result of her sudden vision and viewing of the crucified Messiah (12:10); this oversight will be so startling that it will result in a mighty repentance and national conversion that purges Israel from her idolatry and sin once and for all (vv. 11–14). The prophecy continues to use the first-person pronoun that refers to our LORD as he goes on to tell of that unprecedented moment in history when God moves on behalf of the spiritual needs of the Jewish remnant. Zechariah was not the only prophet to predict this coming event; both Joel and Ezekiel foretold of such a great spiritual visitation upon the Jewish survivors in that future day.

Joel connected such a spiritual revival of the nations with an identical eschatological event:

> "And afterward, I will pour out my Spirit on all people. Your sons and daughters will prophesy, your old men will dream dreams, your young men will see visions. Even on my servants, both men and women, I will pour out my spirit in those days. I will show wonders in the heavens and on earth, blood and fire and billows of smoke. The sun will be turned to darkness and the moon to blood before the coming of the great and dreadful day of the LORD." (Joel 2:28, 29)

Likewise, Ezekiel taught this same truth to be applied to Israel:

> "I will no longer hide my face from them, for I will pour out my Spirit on the people of Israel, declares the Sovereign LORD." (Ezekiel 39:29)

The verb "pour out" (Hebrew *shaphakti*), when used in connection with the Holy Spirit, denotes a copious refreshment, and it is to be received like water falling on thirsty ground. His Spirit will come like a gushing downpour, not just like a light shower!

Israel had seen a momentous day when God won a triumph for the nation of Israel over Pharaoh and his army in Egypt. But an even greater day will be seen when God will triumph not only over the nations gathered to defeat Israel, but also it will be a day when God will triumph over the hearts of the people of Judah in that future day. Few promises of God are more touching and more promising in Scripture.

A huge amount of controversy, nevertheless, rages over the meaning of Zechariah 12:10, for if read literally as it is written, it has huge implications for Israel's future! The New Jewish Publication Society translation of the *Tanakh* in 1985 unfairly rendered this key verse in this manner:

> "But I will fill the house of David and the inhabitants of Jerusalem with a spirit of pity and compassion; and they shall lament to Me about those who are slain, wailing over them as over a favorite son and showing bitter grief as over a first-born."

But the verb used here (*wehibbitu*, "they shall look") is not uncertain or all that difficult to translate from Hebrew into English. Moreover, it is unnatural to suppose that there were two parties in the prophet's mind: the Jewish people who looked on the LORD and the Gentile nations who wailed with cries over the one who was pierced! Even the 1896 Jewish translation had this revised version in an Appendix: "And they (in the house of David and the inhabitants of Jerusalem) shall look up to Me because of Him whom they (i.e., the nations which came against Jerusalem) have pierced." An even more ancient Jewish interpretation surprisingly attributed this prophecy to be about a so-called "Messiah ben Joseph." But such a secondary Messiah does not exist in Scripture; such a Messiah has been invented by the Jewish audience to avoid the direct prophecy set forth in the natural rendering of this verse.

Zechariah 12:10 talks about a coming national Jewish mourning over someone who has stood in an intimate connection with ADONAI and whose rejection and death was bitterly regretted and bewailed by Judah in an unknown future day! Moreover, the wailing on that day will be like the sorrow that went up over the "Hadad Rimmon in the plain of Megiddo" (v. 11). This must have been a reference to the national mourning that the nation Israel experienced over the sudden death of their young good king Josiah at the hands of Pharaoh Necho of Egypt, as Josiah tried in the Megiddo Pass to stop Pharaoh from going to assist Assyria (2 Kgs. 22:29–30; 23:29; 2 Chron. 35:20–27). Hadad-Rimmon is to be identified with a village named Rummaneh, about four miles southeast of Megiddo.

Verses 12–14 identify those who were mourning this one they had looked upon in a whole new way. There were two families named from the royal line (e.g., the family of Nathan was not the family of the prophet Nathan, but rather a reference to another son of David, whose line later on replaced Solomon in the Davidic line of our Lord!) and two families from the priestly line (e.g., the family or "clan of Shimei" was not the Shimei from the tribe of Simeon, but Shimei who was the son of Gershom and the grandson of Levi) (Num. 3:18).

It is clear, however, that in that day, each person in Israel will fully recognize in his or her heart the awfulness of the death and long rejection by the nation of Israel for their Messiah. Each person will mourn apart from each other with almost inconsolable grief and sorrow. But note one more time that the ones looking at the Lord are the ones who pierced him and who now mourn for him.

Zechariah 13:1 declares that on that day, there will be a "fountain" that will be opened for cleansing of all the stored-up sin of each person in the nation of Israel. It will be similar to the cleansing of the High Priest Joshua (Zech. 3:3–5), but there, the High Priest acted as a representative of the whole nation. Here, however, each person in the nation of Israel will come for individual cleansing. This cleansing will remove all "sin" and "impurity" from each repentant Israelite. This event is exactly what the Apostle Paul prayed for in Romans 9–11. At this point in history, the times of the Gentiles will have ended, and it will be time for a repentant Israel to be grafted back into the very same olive tree from which they had been lopped off in unbelief (Rom. 11:26–27). The nation of Israel will now have been washed with the washing of the word and renewed by the inner work of the Holy Spirit (Titus 3:5).

Conclusions

1. When Messiah returns the second time, he will come in clouds and every eye shall see him (Rev. 1:7). This will be an open event seen by all and not a secret event!

2. The Lord will conquer the nations of the earth that ruthlessly gather to end the Jewish existence on the planet. God will affect an astonishing deliverance, which will benefit the embattled nation of Israel.

3. The city of Jerusalem will be so immovable that all who attempt to move it will herniate themselves in their attempt to do so.

4. Our Lord is able to conquer the hearts of Israel and the nations just as well as he is more than able to confront all the armament of all who oppose him; however, this time he will capture the hearts of Israel so that their long opposition to him will cease as a great national repentance takes place and all Israel is saved in that day.

Lesson 14

Cleansing the Land and Gathering the Scattered Sheep

Zechariah 13:2–9

There is little doubt that the opening six verses of Zechariah 13 stand in closest relationship to the prophecy of chapter 12. As such, it is a mirror image of the message of the first burden; for example, in 13:2–6 the prophet scolds the false prophets as he did in 12:2–6. In those days, there did not seem to be any shortage of false or counterfeit prophets.

The Old Testament does not use the specific term "false prophet(s)," but it is clear that such "professional prophets," who were fakes, existed during much of Israel's history. It was the Septuagint (Greek translators) that introduced the term *pseudoprophetes*, "false prophet," ten times, where the Hebrew merely used *nabi*, "prophet" (Jer. 6:13; 26:7–8, 11, 16; 27:9; 28:1; 29:1, 8; Zech. 13:2). These false prophets were diametrically opposed to what the canonical prophets taught, and often merely imitated what those who were authentic prophets of God taught and copied them even to the extent of imitating what they wore. However, the Hebrew text made its point by using a whole battery of negative terms.

The problem with these prophets of deceit was that they prophesied lies (Jer. 6:13; 27:14; Zech. 13:3), thereby deceiving the people with their own dreams (Jer. 29:8). Moreover, they prophesied on the alleged authority of the idol-deity Baal (Jer. 2:8; 23:13), often threatening the very lives of the true prophets of ADONAI (Jer. 26:7). These deceiving prophets had not stood in the council of God to receive their messages (Jer. 28:18); they insisted on promising "peace," but none was to be found (Jer. 6:14; 8:11; 14:3; 23:17; 28:2, 11; Ezek. 13:10; Mic. 3:5). The substance of their prophecies came from their own imaginations and not from God (Jer. 14:14; 23:16; Ezek. 13:2–3; 22:28). Some of these charlatans used magic (Ezek. 13:17–23) to undergird their false messages, while others used divination, soothsaying, witchcraft, necromancy and sorcery—all of which were strongly forbidden per the Torah (Deut. 18:9–13). In fact, these false prophets gave the people the "peace" message they wanted to hear, and they had the ability to also "whitewash" any situation with false optimism, no matter how discouraging or adverse the situation really was (Ezek. 13:10–12, 14–15; 22:28).

The prophet Jeremiah gave the fullest discussion of the charges brought against the false prophets (Jer. 23:9–39). He leveled four charges against these pompous pretenders: (1) They were men of immoral character (23:14; for they "they commit[ed] adultery and live[d] a lie"); (2) they sought popular acclaim by advocating an unconditional pledge of immunity for their hearers from all imminent disasters (23:17–22); (3) they didn't distinguish their own dreams from true words from God (23:25–29); and (4) they were plagiarists who stole from each other words they alleged were from God (23:30–39). They claimed to have received a "burden" from the Lord, but really, they themselves were a "burden" the Lord had to deal with.

The theology of these false prophets involved their being super advocates of a nationalism, as they were overzealous to maintain, on the wrong basis, Zion/Jerusalem's invincibility and inviolability. They stressed the permanence of David's dynasty, the endurance of the Temple, and the steadfastness of the covenant God made with Abraham, Isaac, Jacob and David—a guarantee that operated on without fail for every generation! So certain were they about the promises made by God at Sinai that he would be Israel's God, and Israel would be his people, that this allowed for a lot of leeway in their acting and loose living. All alleged revelations from God, they taught, such as predictions of judgment, doom, disaster and expressions of his wrath, were contrary to their list of immutable expectations. They taught all such negative declarations were wrong because they were treasonous and outside the description of who God was as a loving Lord.

Scripture gave five criteria for testing if a prophet was false or true (Deut. 13:1–5; 18:15–22). A true prophet of God must (1) be Jewish—"of your brethren" (18:18); (2) he must announce his prophecies in the name of the LORD (18:19–20); (3) he must show by his immediate or near-happening predictions that his long-range or distant prophecies were thus also reliable (18:21–22); (4) he must be able to show signs and wonders (miracles) along with his prophecies (13:1–2a); and (5) his messages must conform to what God previously had revealed in his word (13:2b–5). All too often, the false prophet prophesied in the name of one of his false gods, which that prophet syncretized with ADONAI's name and the name of his god (Jer. 23:13, 17, 25; 26:27). In these cases, the fraudulent nature of their predictions was more apparent, but in other cases it was harder to tell whether this was a true or false prophecy. For example, in the case of the unnamed prophet who came from Judah to give a true divine word to King Jeroboam in the north. His prophecy showed its immediate truthfulness as the altar on which the king was sacrificing burst open, and the ashes rolled out of the altar as the true prophet of God claimed they would (1 Kgs. 13). But that same true prophet later disobeyed God by returning to the site up north where he had ministered so courageously for the Lord at the improper pleading of a northern prophet, who announced that he too was a true prophet of God; that same false prophet later would give a true word from God that would be fulfilled in the life and experience of the prophet who had come from the south to deliver the true word of God to the northern kingdom. That new word from God was realized when the prophet from the south died from his wounds after being mauled by a lion that met him as he went south to his home, as had been predicted by the old prophet of that city (1 Kgs. 13:20–22). Thus, not everything a prophet said was inspired! Only that which had the authority of the word of God behind it was true and reliable; moreover, God never went back on or failed to fulfill his word or commands!

The classic encounter between a true and false prophet in the New Testament came in the incident involving Paul and Barnabas' rebuke given to the Jewish magician Bar-Yeshua on the island of Paphos (Acts 13:6–10). In that case, the Holy Spirit informed Paul that Bar-Yeshua was full of deceit and a false prophet pretending to be otherwise. He, like the pseudo prophets, such as Jezebel at the church of Thyatira (Rev. 2:20), had to be avoided. But it is time we look at the text more closely.

The Fountain Opened for Israel's Cleansing – 13:2–6

In the twelfth chapter of his prophecy, Zechariah depicts the great national repentance and sorrow over the One they had "pierced" (12:10). Therefore, the first six verses of chapter 13 are closely tied to the magnificent prophecy in chapter 12.

The work of the Holy Spirit will result in a spiritual cleansing 13:1. Such a cleansing has already been illustrated in this book with the cleansing seen in Zechariah 3:3–5, as the High Priest Joshua has his filthy clothes removed and exchanged for new ones. Consequently, in this text, there is the promise of a "fountain" that will be "opened," which points to the fact that such a cleansing will be available for a good period of time. Whereas the wells for such cleansing may have been stopped up and blocked for some time, this fountain will continue to be opened for individuals' cleansing. This is the same cleansing that the prophet Ezekiel had promised would be available for cleansing (Ezek. 36:25–28), which seems well in accord with the same provisions contained in the New Covenant (Jer. 31:31–34).

Those who would benefit from this cleansing from the fountain are here identified as "the house of David" and the "inhabitants of Jerusalem." These, according to Zechariah 12:10–11, represent the whole nation of

Israel—the Jewish people! This cleansing will result in the removal of "sin" and "impurity," constituting a failure to meet God's standard, a missing of the mark, and a failure to be ritually and ceremonially fit for the worship of God respectfully. Therefore, Israel had deviated from God's moral and ceremonial standards. It is a fountain of cleansing water, not a fountain filled with "blood," as William Cowper wrote in a 1771 poem.

The shed blood of Messiah is the basis for the cleansing itself, which the prophet graphically portrays. Thus the fountain is filled with water, not blood!

The penitential sorrow of Israel will come in that future day from seeing the One whom they have pierced (12:10). But the repentance that will come "in that day," as the iniquity of the land is removed as if it were in "one day" (3:9), will come so suddenly and will be so widespread that it will be as if a cistern or spring had suddenly been opened and a nation was born all at once in repentance and in recognition of their Messiah!

The two chief sources of moral pollution in Israel were idolatry and false prophecy. But in that day, the Lord will completely purge Israel of these two evils as he cuts off the names of the idols in the land and causes the false prophets to pass out of the land (13:2). The eyes of Israel that had formerly been spiritually blind will now be opened to see, for the first time, the Lamb of God who had offered himself as an atonement for the sins of all who would believe in Him. The fountain of cleansing will not only be opened, but it shall remain open and accessible to all who will trust him as Savior and as a fount of cleansing from their sin. Likewise, "the spirit of impurity/uncleanness," which is in direct contrast to the "Holy Spirit" (12:10) will be exterminated from the land of Israel.

What now follows in vv. 3–6 is an expansion of what is stated in v. 2, where idolatry and false prophecy will be banished from the land forever. Verse 3 begins with a hypothetical illustration of what is announced in v. 2. It begins with an allusion to Deuteronomy 13:6–10, where a family member, or even a close relative, might attempt to entice another member of the family, or even a close friend, to serve other gods, but for that deviation from what is true and taught by Scripture, that person is to be put to death. In like manner, if a false prophet were to speak falsely in the name of ADONAI, that prophet must also be put to death (Deut. 18:20).

So serious was the act of prophesying falsely that even if it involved one's own son, who should dare to prophesy so presumptuously, his own parents were to "thrust him through" while he was in the very act of prophesying falsely. The verb used here is the same verb used in 12:10 ("pierced"). One's zeal for the Lord was so strong that in this case it would simply overpower their parental affection otherwise given to this son, for this false prophet, who was one of their own children, must be put to death! In fact, the day is coming when such pretended prophets will be ashamed of any so-called visions they might offer. When asked about the wounds that appear on the body of this prophet, "between [his] hands," and when they would be pressed to know if such wounds had come from the frantic slashing of his own body with knives (2 Kgs. 18:28) or from other sorts of antics that go with Baal and Canaanite worship, he will deny all the above. Instead, he will deceitfully claim these wounds came from chastisements received in the house of his friends (13:6). The words "between [his] hands" refers most likely to his chest; and the word for "friends" may be rendered more accurately "my lovers." Even the "hairy garment," which he had made of camel's hair for himself, or from untanned skins, such as was worn by John the Baptist or the prophet Elijah, was abandoned and no longer worn by these pretenders. Such a garment was a "cloak of hypocrisy" worn to deceive their gullible listeners. Thus, while they may have outwardly looked like true prophets of God, inwardly they were "raving wolves." They were not to be tolerated in Israel; these frauds were to be eradicated!

The Death of Messiah for Israel's National Cleansing – 13:7a, b

Once again, we return to the shepherd motif found in chapter 11 as this verse begins a new section. This one is very significant, for it depicts the judgment that will fall on Jerusalem at the hands of the ungodly. But these ungodly invaders will be cut off as the righteous remnant and the land of Israel is purified and made ready to be the center of God's kingdom on earth. This will be done in two parts. The first, in 13:7–9, will summarize the contents; the second, in 14:1–21, will expand on this event in greater detail.

Now, in a vivid personification, the "sword" is addressed as an instrument of death, as it is instructed to move against the shepherd. Herein lies one of the greatest of mysteries: The sword will move against the One who is absolutely innocent. The Lord indeed calls this shepherd "my shepherd," indicating this is no ordinary shepherd. God also called this shepherd "the man who is close to me" (Hebrew `al geber `amiti, "upon/against the man that is my fellow/nearest one"). This must be more than just high praise; indeed, this shepherd is the one who is side by side with, or even the equal of, the LORD. This could also be interpreted as the "associate" or "companion" to the Lord God. In fact, this whole statement of the equality of the shepherd with the LORD recalls the similar claim in John 10:30 and 14:9. Moreover, it strengthens the case for identifying the "shepherd" of 11:4–14 with the "One who was pierced" in 12:10!

The Deliverance of the Scattered Sheep – 13:7c–9

The sword is told to "Strike the shepherd" (v. 7c), which accords with the same teaching found in Isaiah 53:10 ("Yet it pleased the LORD to bruise him"). So it was that our Lord was delivered up in accordance with the definite plan of God, even though it was mortals who were responsible for the deed and who are culpable for what they did (Acts 2:23).

With the striking of the shepherd, the sheep were scattered. And the cross would continue to be an offense for as long as the Gentile period lasted. Even the "little ones" suffered as the tradition of resisting the significance of Yeshua's awful death was passed on from parents to children.

The people of Israel are here treated as the sheep or flock of God who receive one of earth's most devastating disasters in the end times. "Two-thirds will be struck down and perish" (v. 8b) with only "one-third left in [the land]." It seems that Israel will experience another horror similar to the Holocaust! It will be awful!

However, God will save one-third of Israel. They will be put through the fire and refined just as silver is refined and tested just as gold is tested (v. 9a–c). They will call on the name of the Lord, and he will answer them (v. 9d–e). God will say, "They are my people," and they will reply, "God is our God" (v. 9f–g). Surely, all the impurities will have been refined away in that day.

The Shepherd in 13:7–9 must be our Messiah Yeshua, for who else has such a close relationship to the Father? What will it take, though, for Israel and the nations of the world to recognize who this Shepherd really is and to regard and treat him as such? We are assured that at least one-third of Israel will come to their senses and recognize their long-neglected Messiah—but only after a huge national bloodbath administered from the gathered nations there to oppose and destroy her. Would that more Jewish people—and Gentiles!—come to put their trust in the Messiah even now in these days before the awful days that must be endured in the end-times.

Conclusions

1. There is a fountain filled with the cleansing water of the word of God and the forgiving mercy of our Messiah Yeshua.

2. One day soon Israel as a nation shall look on Yeshua whom they have pierced and suddenly be smitten with the reality of what they have done as they mourn over such an event as they have never mourned before. Israel should have plunged into that cleansing fountain a long time ago!

3. Through Israel's mourning, she will experience spiritual repentance, renewal and restoration with her Lord.

4. It is an awesome responsibility to deliver the word of God without toying with it, distorting it or twisting it to fit some idea or loyalty we might have from sources other than the word of God. False prophets are more serious a matter than a plague of some disease, for these prophets can mislead a person so that mortals are deceived away from the path to everlasting life and the joy in fellowship with the Savior and their lives destroyed for all eternity.

5. The twofold nature of Messiah is brought out in this passage: He is "man" according to his human nature and "God" according to his divine nature.

6. Despite the centuries of calling Israel, both in intervening actions and in the power of the word of God, Israel still by and large has refused all these years to repent and accept their Messiah.

7. The nations think they can eradicate Israel from the face of the earth, but God will step in once more to deliver one-third of them that are left as he returns to set up his reign that will last forever.

Lesson 15

Preparing for God's Glorious Consummation of World History

Zechariah 14:1–21

In no other chapter in the Bible is the correct interpretation and identification of the name "Israel" more important than in Zechariah 14. Yet for all too many commentators today, the name "Israel" in this chapter does not represent the people of Judah and Ephraim, i.e., the northern and southern tribes of Israel, but instead "Israel" is often made to represent spiritually or allegorically the Christian Church and not the nation of Israel. This is called "replacement theology" or "supersessionism." Instead of using the usual method of interpreting the text, which takes its literal meaning, these commentators try to give a spiritual or allegorical sense to some of the key words, such as "Israel." But when the text speaks of Israel as experiencing a situation where "two-thirds shall be cut off and die in the land," these interpreters suddenly switch methods and declare that those "cut off" will not be the Christian Church but literal Jews, and the "land" will indeed be the land of Israel in the Near East!

All this discussion over the proper interpretive approach to a chapter like Zechariah 14 is more than a tempest in a teapot! Some commentators unwisely say this chapter defies all historical explanation. Such interpreters have been trying to find some event in the past that would match the events in this chapter, but it made clear it was about the future hopes of the nation of Israel, not any past event or even any of the future hopes of the Christian Church. One cannot start an interpretive process with unrelated general statements alleged to be true from texts found elsewhere in Scripture or ancient literature and then impose that general statement on the particulars of the other text. Many great expositors have rejected the literal interpretation of Zechariah 14. Yet the truth of Messiah's second coming to establish an earthly kingdom over a restored Israel in her land is so frequently emblazoned over the pages of Zechariah and the other prophets that such a deviation and rejection of Israel's identity in these key texts is hard to explain. But now that history is beginning to show that such a lineup of the hostile nations mentioned in these prophesies is beginning to form in the Holy Land, such a rejection is even more inexplicable.

To put the matter more realistically and literally, chapter 14 presents the last siege of Jerusalem by all the nations of the world (vv. 1–3), the personal appearance of Messiah on the Mount of Olives (vv. 4–7), and a portrait of the full kingdom blessings and worship of God at the time of the Feast of Tabernacles (vv. 8–21). But these climactic future episodes have already been presented in 12:1–10, but here they are represented from a slightly different point of view.

The Nations of the World Will Fight Against Jerusalem for the Last Time – 14:1–3

Zechariah 14:1 begins, "A Day of the LORD is coming," which links it with the Old Testament theme of "the day of the LORD." A few commentators deny that this event belongs to the Old Testament theme of the "Day of the LORD." However, the reference here in 14:1 is to "the day of/belonging to the LORD," which occurs here in a most emphatic way. The Hebrew text places a *lamed* before "LORD," thus indicating possession or ownership; thus, it is a day belonging to the LORD par excellence. Moreover, the participle in Hebrew promises that this event in surely "coming," for the participle emphasizes its durative and continuing sense.

The probable course of events that leads up to this crisis in Jerusalem on the day of the LORD includes: (1) The people of Israel will be restored to the land of Canaan in large numbers just prior to the Lord's second coming. (2) After a brief period of prosperity for Israel, then will come one of the nation's darkest days as all of the nations of the world gather against her in a siege (see Zech. 12, 14). (3) Israel will enter into a covenant with one who is otherwise known as the Antichrist, thus Israel will accept any person who comes in his own name, while they reject the name and person of the Lord. (4) The Antichrist will break his covenant (which may be public or secret) with Israel after three-and-a-half years. (5) The nations of the earth will join the Antichrist in their final assault against Israel, saying, "Come, let us cut off the existence of this nation so that it will be remembered no longer." (6) The Lord will intervene on that day, a day like none before or after (cf. Josh. 10:14), and the Lord will be victorious as the "Mighty Man of War."

So, this day is a period that immediately precedes the second coming of the Lord. Indeed, it is a time when the spoil/booty of Israel will be divided among all the nations that come to attack Israel. This will be a time known also as a time of "Jacob's trouble" (Jer. 30:5–7).

It is God himself who gathers all the nations of the world against Israel (v. 2). The prophet Joel had foretold this same event in Joel 3:1–5…

> For behold in those days and at that time, when I bring back the captives of Judah and Jerusalem, I will also gather all nations, and bring them down to the Valley of Jehoshaphat; I will enter into judgment with them there on account of my people, my heritage Israel."

It is clear that the timing of this event will be on the famous "Day of the LORD," referred to elsewhere as "in those days," "at that time," in "that day," the "latter days," or the day when "[God will] restore the fortunes of Judah and Jerusalem" (Joel 3:1). It is also clear that the participants in this siege of Jerusalem will be "all the Nations" of the world. The place will be in the "Valley of Jehoshaphat," or as Revelation 16:13–16 puts it, the battle of Armageddon, which may take place in the plain near the city of Megiddo or in the Kidron Valley, east of Jerusalem. Moreover, there are four reasons why God will enter this battle and bring judgment on the nations of the world: (1) The nations have scattered Israel around the earth (Joel 3:2c). (2) The nations have partitioned the land of Israel (Joel 3:2d). (3) The nations have made slaves of the Jewish people (Joel 3:3). (4) The Babylonians carried off the sacred vessels from the Temple (Joel 3:5).

The horrors of this siege of Jerusalem will be monstrous, for (1) "the city will be captured" (Zech. 14:2b), (2) the "houses rifled/ransacked" (14:2c), (3) the women ravished/raped (14:2d), (4) "half of the city will go into exile" (14:2e), (5) two-thirds of the city will be killed (Zech. 13:8b), (6) the remaining one-third of the city will be refined like silver and gold are refined, but they "will not be taken from the city" (Zech. 14:2f, 13:8c, 9a–c).

Then the LORD will say, in effect: "Enough already!" (Zech. 14:3a); he will enter the battle and fight as he has fought in the memorable battles of Gideon (Judg. 7:21–22) or Jehoshaphat (2 Chron. 20). This entrance of the LORD into the battle will come at just the moment when the Antichrist and his world forces seem to have gained the upper hand in that ultimate battle, with only a third in Jerusalem left to fight. God will "go forth" as the "Man of War" (Ex. 15:3) and fight magnificently for Israel.

Messiah Will Appear a Second Time on Earth – 14:4–7

Messiah will touch down on earth on the Mount of Olives, perhaps on the very spot where he had spoken to those who were at the Mount when he ascended to heaven. The angels who accompanied him at that time said:

> Men of Galilee, why [are] you stand[ing] [here] gazing up into heaven? This same Yeshua, who was taken up from you into heaven, will so come in like manner as you saw him go into heaven. (Acts 1:11).

Here, on the Mount of Olives, where Yeshua left Jerusalem, is the place where he would return in the same manner as he left. This prediction accords well with the prophecy that Ezekiel gave. The Glory of the LORD, which symbolized his very presence, left the Temple in Jerusalem, and crossed over to the Mount of Olives, where the Glory of the LORD ascended to heaven and will not return until Messiah returns to earth. Then his name will be the "LORD is there," or to say it in Hebrew: "*ADONAI Shammah!*" (Ezek. 10:4, 18–19; 11:22–24; 43:1–5; 48:35b).

When our Lord touches down on the Mount of Olives, there will be an enormous earthquake that will split the Mount of Olives east to west. The best-known fault line begins north of the Sea of Galilee and continues down the Jordan River Valley through the Dead Sea all the way down the Nile River Valley to Victoria Falls at the equator. But another fault-line was recently discovered through the Mount of Olives. That newly formed valley shall reach all the way to Azel. This may be the same place alluded to in Micah 1:11, known as Beth-Azel. So strong will this earthquake be, apparently having a worldwide impact, that it will remind all in Israel of the earthquake that came in the days of Uzziah, king of Judah, an event still well remembered. Josephus related this catastrophe to Uzziah's attempt to offer incense in the Temple of the LORD against the protests of the priests of Israel.

On that day, the celestial luminaries will also cease to function; there will be "neither sunlight nor cold, [just] frosty darkness" (14:6). Was this what Isaiah meant as he said: "See, the day of the LORD is coming. ... The stars of heaven and their constellations will not show their light. The rising sun will be darkened, and the moon will not give its light" (24:23; cf. Joel 3:14–16; Mt. 24:29–30; Mk. 13:24–25; Rev. 6:13; 8:12)? This will be a day like none the earth has ever known. But there will no longer be a need for the light of these celestial bodies, for the resplendent light of the glory of God's presence will be reflected over the earth. A whole new order of creation will have dawned, the glory of which will far exceed the light of the prior creation!

Messiah's Kingdom Will Be Established Over the Whole World – 14:8–15

Most important of all, "The LORD shall be king over all the earth" (14:9), for then it will happen just as Revelation 11:15b says: "The kingdoms of this world [will] become the kingdoms of our LORD and of his Messiah, and he shall reign forever and ever!" Yeshua the Messiah will be acknowledged as "King of kings and Lord of lords" worldwide (Rev. 19:16). Add to this the fact that "The LORD is one, and his name one"

(14:9b). In that future day, our Lord will be acknowledged as the only Lord with no rivals whatsoever—he is our incomparably great Lord!

In paradise restored (Rev. 22:1), there will issue forth from the entrance to the sanctuary a life-giving stream of water (14:8b–c), in which one half will flow to "eastern sea," the Dead Sea, and one half to the "western sea," the Mediterranean. This flow of water will never stop. It will even flow out to the entire desert region of the Jordan (Ezek. 47:1–12). The prophet Joel had seen such a day when all the brooks and streams of Judah would flow full of water and a fountain would come from the house of the Lord (3:18).

More, the peace of Jerusalem will never again be disturbed (14:11). And to accommodate Jerusalem's new status as the religious and governmental capital of the world, the uplifted plain will give a whole new landscape to the terrain from the massive quake. Jerusalem itself will be uplifted and inhabited from Benjamin's gate on the north wall (perhaps the "Gate of Ephraim" in 2 Kgs. 14:3), to the "First Gate" on the northeast corner of the city, on to the "Corner Gate" on the northwest corner on to the "Tower of Hananeel," perhaps in the southeast corner of Jerusalem on the south side of the city near the Valley of Hinnom. No longer would there be a "curse," or "sentence of destruction," on the people of the city (Hebrew *herem*).

The beautiful picture of salvation and joy found in vv. 8–12 has its obverse in vv. 12–15. God will inflict on his enemies the judgment and punishment he had promised to all who walk contrary to his will and law.

Three weapons will be used by God in order to deal with the enemies of his plan and of his person: a deadly plague (v. 12), a mutual annihilation on one another among the enemies themselves as a consequence of a great panic that will come from the LORD (v. 13), and a superhuman valor that comes upon the remnant of Judah, who will take up the fight in Jerusalem at this final day (v. 14). In reality, vv. 12–15 follow Zechariah 14:1–3 in actual happenings, for they are an amplification and a supplement to what is found in vv. 1–3 and 12:4–10. As Zechariah did not want to interrupt the sequence of events that would describe the magnificent deliverance of the people of God in Israel, he finished first that joyous news before reverting to the issue of the necessary judgment that would befall all who opposed Messiah.

The word for "plague" (*nagaph*, "to strike, smite") is from the same Hebrew root as the word "plague," a "blow," a fatal "stroke." This is the same word used for the divinely sent "plague" against Pharaoh (Ex. 9:14). But as used here, this plague is unprecedented in its severity and terribleness. The nations will be hit hard for their virulent anti-Semitism as seen in the seven last plagues in Revelation 15:1, in which bowls are filled with the wrath of God (Rev. 16:1–21).

In a more graphic manner, the penalty of this plague will come again against all the nations that have come to attack Jerusalem. The Lord will make their flesh suddenly to "rot" while they are standing on their feet (12b). In Hebrew, "rot" is *maqaq*, which means "to fester" because of the wounds given to them as a punishment for their iniquity. Likewise, their eyes will "rot" in their sockets and their tongues will also "rot." This rotten outbreak will be immediate and evidently while the battle is in progress. Never before has humanity experienced anything like what will happen in this battle, for the divine visitation of his wrath will be so sudden that the wicked tongues that had previously blasphemed God will in an instant be silenced! A similar plague would strike the horses, mules, camels and donkeys, and all the animals in the enemy's camps (v. 15).

When a whole city commits the crime of idolatry, in accordance with the law of *herem*, the "ban," results not only in the fact that all the inhabitants were put to death, but the animals too. An instance of this can be seen in the case of Achan, whose oxen, asses, and sheep were stoned and burned along with the humans involved in taking a dedicated or consecrated find among the heathen (Josh. 7:24–25).

In addition to this deadly plague that will befall Israel's attackers in earth's final battle, another divine weapon will be unleashed against the hapless nations. This will be a great and fearful "commotion" (Hebrew *mehumah*, "tumult, disturbance") or "wild panic" that somehow enters the battle scene. In this ensuing wild disturbance, every attacker will suddenly start slaughtering each other, similar to previous events where God confounded the foes of Israel by causing those who rose up against Israel to start slaughtering each other. A good example of such an action can be seen in Gideon's victory with his 300 (Judg. 7:22), Jonathan's magnificent triumph over the Philistines at Michmash (I Sam. 14:14–16), or Jehoshaphat's victory over three nations (Ammon, Moab, Mount Seir) who clearly outnumbered his forces by a wide margin (2 Chron. 20).

A third divinely implemented weapon was the superhuman valor God suddenly gifted the remnant of Israel. They rose to the occasion in a way they had not exerted in the battle up to this point. As a result of their extermination of the confederated forces that had opposed them in Jerusalem, "the wealth of the nations" would be harvested by Israel in "great abundance," i.e., their gold, silver and apparel.

Jerusalem Will Serve as the Religious Center of the World – 14:16–21

The judgment of God had a deleterious effect on the nations, for all the ones left among those that came up against Jerusalem will make it a habit to go up to Jerusalem at the time of the Feast of Tabernacles each year to worship the Lord as King of Kings (v. 16). Thus, year after year in the future, all the families and nations of earth will go to Jerusalem to worship God.

But why has the prophet Zechariah singled out the Feast of Tabernacles, from all the other festivals, as the event that must be honored representatively each year by all the nations? Even the Jewish Mishnah and the Talmud singled out this Feast of Tabernacles/Booths from all the other feasts as having a prophetic character and one that was in anticipation of what was to come (Lev. 23:39, 42–43; Deut. 16:13–16). Nothing that has happened in history answers the meaning of the Feast of Tabernacles. Thus its fulfillment must still come. After the national Day of Atonement takes place one day in the future, the nation that had originally been chosen to be a light to the nations, i.e., Israel, will channel blessings to the world after they have been cleansed, reconciled and equipped by the knowledge and power of Messiah. That nation shall be God's instrument over the whole earth for the "Feast of Ingathering," as all peoples shall sit down to feast on all the fruits of the harvest, which ADONAI has prepared on Mount Zion.

This feast was also known as the Feast of Ingathering (Ex. 23:16; 34:22; Deut. 16:13), for it celebrated not only the full ingathering of the labors from the fields of that year but also all the fruit and vintage that could now be harvested. In later times, the Rabbis referred to this Feast as *Sukkoth*, "tabernacles, booths." In these temporary booths or tabernacles they dwelt for that week of celebration. They also associated it with the cloud of glory that hovered over the tabernacle itself.

It will be necessary for all nations to appear before ADONAI each year at Jerusalem (17). Should any nation decide they will not go up to Jerusalem, the Lord will withhold the rain from them (v. 17c). This had been the method in the past of reminding the nations that, should they become apostate, then God would shut off the rain to their crops (Lev. 16:19–20; Deut. 28:24; 1 Kgs. 17:1; Hag. 1:11).

Egypt is singled out as an instance of a nation that might choose to not go up to Jerusalem to worship the Lord (v. 18), as they had grown accustomed to depending on the Nile River to flood their lands for centuries prior to 1970 and the building of the Aswan Dam. But the LORD will inflict a plague on Egypt and any other nations that might choose a similar path of disobedience. Even when the LORD God, as King of the universe, was present on earth, it will still be important to worship him. Verse 19 calls for a punishment on all who do not celebrate the Festival of Tabernacles.

On that final day, notes the final two verses (20–21) of this fourteenth chapter, the aim and purpose of the whole law was finally realized in the climax of this festival and the work of God through all the previous years: holiness to the LORD. While so many had been in bondage to the penalty of the law, they could now attain what previously had been unattainable: God would write his law on their inward parts and write it on their hearts. Then the world would see for the first time the magnificent result of a whole nation with every individual consecrated totally to the Lord. Holiness would not only be written on every person, but everything they possessed would be "Holy to the LORD." In that day, no longer would such distinctions as "profane," "most holy" or "secular" persist; all such distinctions would completely cease in that day. Such a distinction between holy and profane/secular were necessary only when there was sin and moral defilement, but God will utterly remove all these and wipe them away.

Finally, there will not even be the need for a "Canaanite," or as better translated, a "merchant" or "trader" (v. 21c). Whether this term stands for an unclean Canaanite or a godless merchant, the point is this: Nothing will be there in that day that defiles, makes an abomination, disturbs the peace, or mars the holiness of the Lord. God's house will be holy to the Lord, and so will the people!

Conclusions

1. The day of the LORD will bring both the most awful final battle against Israel and the most glorious deliverance ever seen on earth.

2. Yeshua will return in the clouds and touch down on the Mount of Olives. In response to his coming, the Mount of Olives will split east and west, with half moving north and the other half of the mountain moving south.

3. Yeshua will be King over the whole earth in that day, and his rule and reign will know no end; it will be everlasting!

4. The terrors connected with the final battle are awesome, for they will include three great woes: a plague that will strike all nations, a panic that will grip the nations as they turn to fight each other, and the armies of Judah suddenly will be armed with almost superhuman power as the battle immediately is reversed and the Jewish people are victorious.

5. The Feast of Tabernacles will be held each year in Jerusalem with the attendance of all nations required and backed with a penalty for non-compliance.

6. The aim and purpose of the law will finally be reached in that day. Everything and everyone who survived will be "holy to the LORD."

Printed in the United States
by Baker & Taylor Publisher Services